Filling Up the Afflictions
of Christ

Other Books in
The Swans Are Not Silent Series

The Legacy of Sovereign Joy
The Hidden Smile of God
The Roots of Endurance
Contending for Our All

Other Books by John Piper

God's Passion for His Glory

The Pleasures of God

Desiring God

The Dangerous Duty of Delight

Future Grace

A Hunger for God

Let the Nations Be Glad!

A Godward Life

Pierced by the Word

Seeing and Savoring Jesus Christ

The Misery of Job and the Mercy of God

The Innkeeper

The Prodigal's Sister

Recovering Biblical Manhood and Womanhood

What's the Difference?

The Justification of God

Counted Righteous in Christ

Brothers, We Are Not Professionals

The Supremacy of God in Preaching

Beyond the Bounds
(with Justin Taylor)

Don't Waste Your Life

The Passion of Jesus Christ

Life as a Vapor

A God-Entranced Vision of All Things (with Justin Taylor)

When I Don't Desire God

Sex and the Supremacy of Christ
(with Justin Taylor)

Taste and See

Fifty Reasons Why Jesus Came to Die

God Is the Gospel

What Jesus Demands from the World

Amazing Grace in the Life of William Wilberforce

Battling Unbelief

Suffering and the Sovereignty of God
(with Justin Taylor)

50 Crucial Questions

When the Darkness Will Not Lift

The Future of Justification

The Supremacy of Christ in a Postmodern World
(with Justin Taylor)

Spectacular Sins

Finally Alive: What Happens When We Are Born Again

John Calvin and His Passion for the Majesty of God

Rethinking Retirement

This Momentary Marriage: A Parable of Permanence

Stand: A Call for the Endurance of the Saints (with Justin Taylor)

Velvet Steel

the swans are not silent

BOOK FIVE

Filling *up the* AFFLICTIONS *of* CHRIST

The Cost of Bringing the Gospel to the
Nations in the Lives of William Tyndale,
Adoniram Judson, and John Paton

JOHN PIPER

CROSSWAY BOOKS
WHEATON, ILLINOIS

Hardcover ISBN: 978-1-4335-1046-5

ISBN PDF: 978-1-4335-1047-2

ISBN Mobipocket: 978-1-4335-1048-9

Library of Congress Cataloging-in-Publication Data
Piper, John, 1946-
   Filling up the afflictions of Christ : the cost of bringing the gospel to the nations in the lives of William Tyndale, Adoniram Judson, and John Paton / John Piper.
      p. cm. — (The swans are not silent; bk. 5)
   Includes bibliographical references and indexes.
   ISBN 978-1-4335-1046-5 (hc)
     1. Paton, John Gibson, 1824–1907. 2. Missionaries—Vanuatu—Biography. 3. Missionaries—Scotland—Biography. 4. Judson, Adoniram, 1788–1850. 5. Missionaries—Burma—Biography. 6. Missionaries—United States—Biography. 7. Tyndale, William, d. 1536. 8. Reformation—England—Biography I. Title. II. Series.
BV3700.P56   2009
266.0092'2—dc22   2009001557

LB		18	17	16	15	14	13	12	11	10	09
14	13	12	11	10	9	8	7	6	5	4	3	2

To those who suffer
to spread the gospel
"Remember those who are in prison,
as though in prison with them,
and those who are mistreated,
since you also are in the body."
HEBREWS 13:3

CONTENTS

A letter from John Calvin to five young Frenchmen about to be martyred in 1553 for carrying the gospel into France:

We who are here shall do our duty in praying that He would glorify Himself more and more by your constancy, and that He may, by the comfort of His Spirit, sweeten and endear all that is bitter to the flesh, and so absorb your spirits in Himself, that in contemplating that heavenly crown, you may be ready without regret to leave all that belongs to this world.

Now, at this present hour, necessity itself exhorts you more than ever to turn your whole mind heavenward. As yet, we know not what will be the event. But, since it appears as though God would use your blood to seal His truth, there is nothing better for you than to prepare yourselves for that end, beseeching Him so to subdue you to His good pleasure, that nothing may hinder you from following whithersoever He shall call. . . . Since it pleases Him to employ you to the death in maintaining His quarrel, He will strengthen your hands in the fight and will not suffer a single drop of your blood to be shed in vain.

Your humble brother, John Calvin

PREFACE

This is the fifth book in a collection called "The Swans Are Not Silent." By *swans* I mean the inspiring lives of faithful Christians in history. They are *not silent* in the sense that their lives still speak powerfully for our encouragement and guidance.

The terminology of *swans not being silent* comes from the story of St. Augustine's retirement as the Bishop of Hippo in North Africa in A.D. 430. He was one of the greatest voices for biblical truth in the history of the Christian church. When Eraclius, his humble successor, preached at the retirement celebration, he said, "The cricket chirps, the swan is silent."

When I first read that years ago, I said, *No, Eraclius, the swans are not silent.* They go on speaking. That is, they continue speaking, *if* someone tells their story and gives them a voice. That is what I am trying to do with these stories—fifteen of them now (three in each book).

One of the most sobering discoveries of my life is that God spreads the life-giving news about Jesus Christ by means of suffering and martyrdom. That's what the lives of William Tyndale, Adoniram Judson, and John Paton illustrate. They were living—and dying—examples of Colossians 1:24: "I rejoice in my sufferings for your sake, and in my flesh I am filling up what is lacking in Christ's afflictions for the sake of his body, that is, the church."

Afflictions are not merely the *result* of missionary fruitfulness, but also the *means*. God has appointed our pain to be part of his powerful display of the glory of Christ. The worth of Jesus in the world shines more brightly in the lives of those who say by their sacrificial lives, "I have suffered the loss of all things and count them as rubbish, in order that I may gain Christ" (Philippians 3:8).

Few things inspire me to live radically for Christ more than the story of those who did. I pray that this will be the effect on you as well. The nations are in desperate need. And Christ is a great Savior.

ACKNOWLEDGMENTS

I am thankful to Lane Dennis and the team at Crossway for the beautiful work they have done in publishing this series of books called "The Swans Are Not Silent." This is Book Five, and the fruit and fellowship of each volume has been pleasant.

My Executive Pastoral Assistant, David Mathis, encourages and assists and frees me for this work in a way that not only makes it possible but makes it joyful. I thank God for David's proactive thoughtfulness, his theological depth, his biblical faithfulness, his rigorous editing, and his personal friendship.

The elders and staff at Bethlehem Baptist Church continue to support me in ways I don't deserve, encouraging me and covering for me in a hundred ways when I am away finishing a project like this. The church is in good hands. One of these days I will go to heaven instead of going back to the pulpit. They will do just fine. They lean on the One who cannot fail.

Noël and Talitha give me the space and seclusion and prayer I need to work at home. The bond we enjoy is deep. I am who I am because of those I am bound to—especially Jesus and my family. O how thankful I am that this bond is life-sustaining, not life-destroying.

Finally, in this book especially, I thank God that he is "near to the brokenhearted and saves the crushed in spirit." Where would we be if we could not say of him, "Many are the afflictions of the righteous, but the LORD delivers him out of them all" (Psalm 34:18–19)?

INTRODUCTION

Tears of Blood to Bless the World

The Lord Jesus said to us in very sobering words, "Truly, truly, I say to you, unless a grain of wheat falls into the earth and dies, it remains alone; but if it dies, it bears much fruit" (John 12:24). Then he added this: "Whoever loves his life loses it, and whoever hates his life in this world will keep it for eternal life" (John 12:25).

In other words, a fruitful life and an eternal life come from dying like a seed and hating your life in this world. What overwhelms me, as I ponder this and trace the lives of William Tyndale, John Paton, and Adoniram Judson, is how strategic it was that they died so many times and in so many ways before their lives on earth ended. This is no rhetorical flourish. The Bible speaks this way, and these followers of Christ knew it.

For example, when John Paton was celebrating the triumphs of the gospel on the island of Tanna in the New Hebrides, after long missionary labor and suffering, he traced this victory back to the fact that "seeds of faith and hope were planted not only in tears, but tears of blood."[1] Then to give biblical force to what he had just said. he simply cited the amazing phrase from 2 Corinthians 11:23 where Paul described his sufferings with the words "in deaths oft." That is the old King James Version and is exactly literal.

---

[1]John G. Paton, *Missionary to the New Hebrides: An Autobiography Edited by His Brother* (1889, 1891; reprint, Edinburgh: The Banner of Truth, 1965), p. 221.

Paul said in 1 Corinthians 15:31, "I die every day!" The seed falls into the ground and dies not just once in martyrdom, but over and over as we obey the command to take up our cross "daily" and follow Jesus (Luke 9:23).

God's Painful Path to Reach All Peoples

More and more I am persuaded from Scripture and from the history of missions that God's design for the evangelization of the world and the consummation of his purposes includes the suffering of his ministers and missionaries. To put it more plainly and specifically, God designs that the suffering of his ambassadors is one essential means in the triumphant spread of the Good News among all the peoples of the world.

I am saying more than the obvious fact that suffering is a *result* of faithful obedience in spreading the gospel. That is true. Jesus said suffering will result from this faithfulness. "You will be hated by all for my name's sake" (Luke 21:17). "If they persecuted me, they will also persecute you" (John 15:20). I am saying that this suffering is part of God's strategy for making known to the world who Christ is, how he loves, and how much he is worth.

This is both frightening and encouraging. It frightens us because we know that we may very likely be called to suffer in some way in order to get the breakthrough we long to see in a hard frontline missions situation. But it also encourages us because we can know that our suffering is not in vain and that the very pain that tends to dishearten us is the path to triumph, even when we can't see it. Many have gone before us on the Calvary Road of suffering and proved by their perseverance that fruit follows the death of humble seeds.

Jesus came into the world to suffer and die for the salvation of a countless number of believers from all the peoples of the world. "The Son of Man came not to be served but to serve, and to give his life as a ransom for many" (Mark 10:45). "By your blood you ransomed people for God from every tribe and language and people and nation" (Revelation 5:9).

Suffering and death in the place of sinners was the way that Christ accomplished salvation. "Christ redeemed us from the curse of the law by becoming a curse for us" (Galatians 3:13). "He was wounded for our transgressions; he was crushed for our iniquities" (Isaiah 53:5). We preach that. It is the heart of the gospel.

But this voluntary suffering and death to save others is not only the *content* but it is also the *method* of our mission. We proclaim the Good News of what he accomplished, and we join him in the Calvary method. We embrace his sufferings *for* us, and we spread the gospel by our suffering *with* him. As Joseph Tson puts it in his own case: "I am an extension of Jesus Christ. When I was beaten in Romania, He suffered in my body. It is not my suffering: I only had the honor to share His sufferings."[2] Pastor Tson goes on to say that Christ's suffering is for *propitiation*; our suffering is for *propagation*. In other words, when we suffer with him in the cause of missions, we display the way Christ loved the world and in our own sufferings extend his to the world. This is what it means to fill up the afflictions of Christ (Colossians 1:24).

First Bible, Then Biography

The plan of this book is to focus first on some of the Scriptures that support these claims (the Introduction) and

---

[2]Joseph Tson, "A Theology of Martyrdom" (an undated booklet of The Romanian Missionary Society, Wheaton, IL), p. 4.

then to let the lives of Tyndale, Paton, and Judson give these Scriptures a flesh-and-blood reality. Among thousands of devoted and faithful missionaries in the history of world missions, Tyndale, Judson, and Paton are not the only ones who display this truth.

In fact, we will, no doubt, find out in heaven that many of the most faithful and fruitful missionaries are almost completely unknown, except in the all-important books of heaven. But the lives of some have been recorded on earth. I am thankful for this. They are a source of great strength to me. That's why I read about their lives. Among those whose lives are recorded for us, few are more heartbreakingly inspiring than the lives of Tyndale, Paton, and Judson. With the thousands of others, these three show how the advance of the gospel of Christ comes about not only through the faithful proclamation of the truth, but also through filling up the afflictions of Christ.

God's Plan for the Nations of the World

The invincible purpose of God in history is that "the gospel of the glory of Christ" (2 Corinthians 4:4) spread to all the peoples of the world and take root in God-centered, Christ-exalting churches. This was the promise of the Old Testament:

> All the ends of the earth shall remember
> and turn to the LORD,
> and all the families of the nations shall worship
>   before you.
> For kingship belongs to the LORD,
> and he rules over the nations. (Psalm 22:27–28)

It was the promise of Jesus to his disciples:

> And this gospel of the kingdom will be proclaimed through-
> out the whole world as a testimony to all nations, and then
> the end will come. (Matthew 24:14)

It was the design of God in the cross, as heaven's worship pro-
claims:

> You were slain, and by your blood you ransomed people for
> God from every tribe and language and people and nation.
> (Revelation 5:9)

It was the final command of the risen, all-authoritative Christ:

> All authority in heaven and on earth has been given to me.
> Go therefore and make disciples of all nations, baptizing
> them in the name of the Father and of the Son and of the
> Holy Spirit, teaching them to observe all that I have com-
> manded you. And behold, I am with you always, to the end
> of the age. (Matthew 28:18–20)

It was the divine aim of Paul's apostleship:

> Through [Christ] we have received grace and apostleship to
> bring about the obedience of faith for the sake of his name
> among all the nations. (Romans 1:5)

It was Paul's holy ambition, rooted not just in a unique apostolic call but also in the Old Testament promise that is still valid
today:

> I make it my ambition to preach the gospel, not where Christ
> has already been named, lest I build on someone else's foun-

dation, but as it is written, "Those who have never been told of him will see, and those who have never heard will understand." (Romans 15:20–21; cf. Isaiah 52:15)

So the Lord has commanded us, saying, "I have made you a light for the Gentiles, that you may bring salvation to the ends of the earth." (Acts 13:47; cf. Isaiah 42:6)

It was the divine purpose of the sending and filling of the Holy Spirit:

You will receive power when the Holy Spirit has come upon you, and you will be my witnesses in Jerusalem and in all Judea and Samaria, and to the end of the earth. (Acts 1:8)

The invincible purpose of God is that "the gospel of the glory of Christ" spread to all the peoples of the world and take root in God-centered, Christ-exalting churches. This great global vision of the Christian movement becomes clear and powerful and compelling in the church whenever there is a deep biblical awakening in Christ's people.

This was true in the time of William Tyndale (born 1494) who was captivated by the fervor of the Reformation as God awakened his church to the truth of justification by faith alone. It was true of the generation later when John Paton (born 1824) was part of great stirrings in Scotland that Iain Murray calls "the missionary awakening."[3] And it was true of the time of Adoniram Judson (born 1788) as the Second Great Awakening stirred in America.

---

[3]Iain Murray, *A Scottish Christian Heritage* (Edinburgh: The Banner of Truth, 2006), p. 218. In Chapters 6 and 7 Murray documents the relationship between true gospel awakening and the missionary effect in Scotland.

Your Persecution Is "for a Witness"

The truth that is especially illustrated by the lives of these servants is that God's strategy for breaking through Satan's authority in the world, and spreading the gospel, and planting the church includes the sacrificial suffering of his frontline heralds. Again I emphasize, since it so easily missed, that I am not referring only to the fact that suffering *results* from frontline proclamation. I am referring also to the fact that this suffering is one of God's intended strategies for the success of his mission. Jesus said to his disciples as he sent them out:

> Behold, I am sending you out as sheep in the midst of wolves, so be wise as serpents and innocent as doves. (Matthew 10:16)

There is no doubt what usually happens to a sheep in the midst of wolves. And Paul confirmed the reality in Romans 8:36, quoting Psalm 44:22:

> As it is written, "For your sake we are being killed all the day long; we are regarded as sheep to be slaughtered."

Jesus knew this would be the portion of his darkness-penetrating, mission-advancing, church-planting missionaries. Tribulation, distress, persecution, famine, nakedness, danger, sword (Romans 8:35)—that is what Paul expected, because that is what Jesus promised. Jesus continued:

> Beware of men, for they will deliver you over to courts and flog you in their synagogues, and you will be dragged before

governors and kings for my sake, *to bear witness before them* and the Gentiles. (Matthew 10:17–18)

Notice that the "witness" before governors and kings is not a mere *result* or consequence, but a *design*. Literally: "You will be dragged before . . . kings *for a witness to them* [*eis marturion autois*]." God's design for reaching some governors and kings is the persecution of his people. Why this design for missions? One answer from the Lord Jesus goes like this:

A disciple is not above his teacher, nor a servant above his master. . . . If they have called the master of the house Beelzebul, how much more will they malign those of his household. (Matthew 10:24–25)

Suffering was not just a *consequence* of the Master's obedience and mission. It was the central *strategy* of his mission. It was the way he accomplished our salvation. Jesus calls us to join him on the Calvary Road, to take up our cross daily, to hate our lives in this world, and to fall into the ground like a seed and die, that others might live.

We are not above our Master. To be sure, our suffering does not atone for anyone's sins, but it is a deeper way of doing missions than we often realize. When the martyrs cry out to Christ from under the altar in heaven, "How long before you will judge and avenge our blood?" they are told "to rest a little longer, until the number of their fellow servants and their brothers should be complete, who were to be killed as they themselves had been" (Revelation 6:10–11).

Martyrdom is not the mere consequence of radical love and obedience; it is the keeping of an appointment set in heaven for a certain number: "Wait till the number of martyrs is complete who are to be killed." Just as Christ died to save the unreached peoples of the world, so some missionaries are to die to save the people of the world.

Filling Up the Afflictions of Christ[4]

We would be warranted at this point to be concerned that this way of talking might connect our suffering and Christ's suffering too closely—as though we were fellow redeemers. There is only one Redeemer. Only one death atones for sin—Christ's death. Only one act of voluntary suffering takes away sin. Jesus did this "once for all when he offered up himself" (Hebrews 7:27). "He has appeared once for all at the end of the ages to put away sin by the sacrifice of himself" (Hebrews 9:26). "By a single offering [Christ] *has perfected for all time* those who are being sanctified" (Hebrews 10:14). When he shed his blood, he did it "*once for all,*" having obtained "*eternal* redemption" (Hebrews 9:12). "There is one God, and there is one mediator between God and men, the man Christ Jesus" (1 Timothy 2:5). So there is no doubt that our sufferings add nothing to the atoning worth and sufficiency of Christ's sufferings.

However, there is one verse in the Bible that sounds to many people as if our sufferings are part of Christ's redeeming sufferings. As it turns out, that is not what it means. On the contrary, it is one of the most important verses explaining the thesis of this book—that missionary sufferings are a strategic part of God's plan to reach the nations. The text is Colossians 1:24 where Paul says,

---

[4]The following exposition of Colossians 1:24 depends heavily on the thought and words of my book *Desiring God: Meditations of a Christian Hedonist* (Sisters, OR: Multnomah, 2003), pp. 267–270.

> Now I rejoice in my sufferings for your sake, and in my flesh
> I am filling up what is lacking in Christ's afflictions for the
> sake of his body, that is, the church.

In his sufferings Paul is "filling up what is lacking in Christ's afflictions for . . . the church." What does that mean? It means that Paul's sufferings fill up Christ's afflictions *not* by adding anything to their worth, but by extending them to the people they were meant to save.

What is lacking in the afflictions of Christ is not that they are deficient in worth, as though they could not sufficiently cover the sins of all who believe. What is lacking is that the infinite value of Christ's afflictions is not known and trusted in the world. These afflictions and what they mean are still hidden to most peoples. And God's intention is that the mystery be revealed to all the nations. So the afflictions of Christ are "lacking" in the sense that they are not seen and known and loved among the nations. They must be carried by missionaries. And those missionaries "complete" what is lacking in the afflictions of Christ by extending them to others.

Epaphroditus Gives the Explanation

There is a strong confirmation of this interpretation in the use of similar words in Philippians 2:30. There was a man named Epaphroditus in the church at Philippi. When the church there gathered support for Paul (perhaps money or supplies or books), they decided to send them to Paul in Rome by the hand of Epaphroditus. In his travels with this supply, Epaphroditus almost lost his life. He was sick to the point of death, but God spared him (Philippians 2:27).

So Paul tells the church in Philippi to honor Epaphroditus when he comes back (v. 29), and he explains his reason with words very similar to Colossians 1:24. He says, "For he nearly died for the work of Christ, risking his life to *complete* [similar word to the one in Colossians 1:24] *what was lacking* [same word as in Colossians 1:24] in your service to me." In the Greek original, the phrase "*complete what was lacking* in your service to me" is almost identical with "*filling up what is lacking* in Christ's afflictions" in Colossians 1:24.

In what sense, then, was the service of the Philippians to Paul "lacking," and in what sense did Epaphroditus "complete" or "fill up" what was lacking in their service? A hundred years ago, Marvin Vincent explained it like this:

> The gift to Paul was a gift of the church as a body. It was a sacrificial offering of love. What was lacking, and what would have been grateful to Paul and to the church alike, was the church's presentation of this offering in person. This was impossible, and Paul represents Epaphroditus as supplying this lack by his affectionate and zealous ministry.[5]

I think that is exactly what the same words mean in Colossians 1:24. Christ has prepared a love offering for the world by suffering and dying for sinners. It is full and lacking in nothing—except one thing, a personal presentation by Christ himself to the nations of the world. God's answer to this lack is to call the people of Christ (people like Paul) to make a personal presentation of the afflictions of Christ to the world.

In doing this, we "complete what is lacking in the afflictions

---

[5]Marvin Vincent, I.C.C., *Epistle to the Philippians and to Philemon* (Edinburgh: T. & T. Clark, 1897), p. 78.

of Christ." We finish what they were designed for, namely, a personal presentation to the people who do not know about their infinite worth.

Filling Up His Afflictions with Our Afflictions

But the most amazing thing about Colossians 1:24 is *how* Paul fills up Christ's afflictions. He says that it is *his own sufferings* that fill up Christ's afflictions. "I rejoice in my sufferings for your sake, and in my flesh I am filling up what is lacking in Christ's afflictions." This means, then, that Paul exhibits the sufferings of Christ by suffering *himself* for those he is trying to win. In *his* sufferings they see Christ's sufferings.

Here is the astounding upshot: *God intends for the afflictions of Christ to be presented to the world through the afflictions of his people.* God really means for the body of Christ, the church, to experience some of the suffering he experienced so that when we proclaim the cross as the way to life, people will see the marks of the cross in us and feel the love of the cross from us. Our calling is to make the afflictions of Christ real for people by the afflictions we experience in bringing them the message of salvation.

The Blood of the Martyrs Is Seed

This is why Paul spoke of his scars as "the marks of Jesus." In his wounds, people could see Christ's wounds. "I bear on my body the marks of Jesus" (Galatians 6:17). The point of bearing the marks of Jesus is that Jesus might be seen and that his love might work powerfully in those who see.

[We] always carr[y] in the body the death of Jesus, so that the life of Jesus may also be manifested in our bodies. For we who live are always being given over to death for Jesus' sake, so that the life of Jesus also may be manifested in our mortal flesh. So death is at work in us, but life in you. (2 Corinthians 4:10–12)

The history of the expansion of Christianity has proved that "the blood of the martyrs is seed," the seed of new life in Christ spreading through the world. That famous quote comes from Tertullian who lived from about A.D. 160 to A.D. 225. What he actually wrote was: "The oftener we are mown down by you [Romans], the more in number we [Christians] grow; the blood of Christians is seed."[6] For almost three hundred years, Christianity grew in soil that was wet with the blood of the martyrs. In his *History of Christian Missions*, Stephen Neil mentions the sufferings of the early Christians as one of the six main reasons the church grew so rapidly.

Because of their dangerous situation vis-à-vis the law, Christians were almost bound to meet in secret. . . . Every Christian knew that sooner or later he might have to testify to his faith at the cost of his life. . . . When persecution did break out, martyrdom could be attended by the utmost possible publicity. The Roman public was hard and cruel, but it was not altogether without compassion; and there is no doubt that the attitude of the martyrs, and particularly of the young women who suffered along with the men, made a deep impression. . . . In the earlier records what we find is calm, dignified, decorous behaviour; cool courage

---

[6]Tertullian, *The Apology*, translated by Rev. S. Thelwell in *Ante-Nicene Fathers, Volume 3, Latin Christianity: Its Founder, Tertullian. I. Apologetic; II. Anti-Marcion; III. Ethical*, ed. Alexander Roberts and James Donaldson (Peabody, MA: Hendrickson Publishers, 2004, originally 1885), p. 55.

in the face of torment, courtesy towards enemies, and a joyful acceptance of suffering as the way appointed by the Lord to lead to his heavenly kingdom. There are a number of well-authenticated cases of conversion of pagans in the very moment of witnessing the condemnation and death of Christians; there must have been far more who received impressions that in the course of time would be turned into a living faith.[7]

May the Lord of the Nations Give Us His Passion

When Paul shares in Christ's sufferings with joy and love, he delivers, as it were, those very sufferings to the ones for whom Christ died. Paul's missionary suffering is God's design to complete the sufferings of Christ, by making them more visible and personal and precious to those for whom he died.

So I say this very sobering word: God's plan is that his saving purpose for the nations will triumph through the suffering of his people, especially his frontline forces who break through the darkness of Satan's blinding hold on an unreached people. That is what the lives of William Tyndale, John Paton, and Adoniram Judson illustrate so dramatically. My prayer is that their stories here will awaken in you a passion for Christ's fame among the nations and sympathy for those who will perish for their sin without having heard the Good News of Christ.

[7]Stephen Neil, A History of Christian Missions (Harmondsworth, Middlesex, UK: Penguin Books Ltd., 1964), pp. 43–44.

1

WILLIAM TYNDALE

"Always Singing One Note"—A Vernacular Bible: The Cost of Bringing the Bible to England

Stephen Vaughan was an English merchant commissioned by Thomas Cromwell, the king's adviser, to find William Tyndale and inform him that King Henry VIII desired him to come back to England out of hiding on the continent. In a letter to Cromwell from Vaughan dated June 19, 1531, Vaughan wrote about Tyndale (1494–1536) these simple words: "I find him always singing one note."[1] That one note was this: Will the King of England give his official endorsement to a vernacular Bible for all his English subjects? If not, Tyndale would not come. If so, Tyndale would give himself up to the king and never write another book.

This was the driving passion of his life—to see the Bible translated from the Greek and Hebrew into ordinary English available for every person in England to read.

Whatever It Costs

Henry VIII was angry with Tyndale for believing and promoting Martin Luther's Reformation teachings. In particular, he was angry because of Tyndale's book *Answer to Sir Thomas*

---

[1]David Daniell, *William Tyndale: A Biography* (New Haven, CT: Yale University Press, 1994), p. 217.

More. Thomas More (famous today for his book *Utopia* and as portrayed in the movie *A Man for All Seasons*) was the Lord Chancellor who helped Henry VIII write his repudiation of Luther called *Defense of the Seven Sacraments.* Thomas More was thoroughly Roman Catholic and radically anti-Reformation, anti-Luther, and anti-Tyndale. So Tyndale had come under excoriating criticism by Thomas More.[2] In fact, More had a "near-rabid hatred"[3] for Tyndale and published three long responses to him totaling nearly three-quarters of a million words.[4]

But in spite of this high-court anger against Tyndale, the king's message to Tyndale, carried by Vaughan, was mercy: "The king's royal majesty is . . . inclined to mercy, pity, and compassion."[5]

The thirty-seven-year-old Tyndale was moved to tears by this offer of mercy. He had been in exile away from his homeland for seven years. But then he sounded his "one note" again: Will the king authorize a vernacular English Bible from the original languages? Vaughan gives us Tyndale's words from May 1531:

> I assure you, if it would stand with the King's most gracious pleasure to grant only a bare text of the Scripture [that is, without explanatory notes] to be put forth among his people, like as is put forth among the subjects of the emperor in these parts, and of other Christian princes, be it of the translation of what person soever shall please his Majesty, I shall immediately make faithful promise never to write more, nor abide two days in these parts after the same: but immediately to repair unto his realm, and there most humbly submit myself at the feet of his royal majesty,

---

[2]For example, in More's 1529 book *Dialogue Concerning Heresies.*
[3]Daniell, *Tyndale,* p. 4.
[4]Thomas More wrote vastly more to condemn Tyndale than Tyndale wrote in defense. After one book called *An Answer unto Sir Thomas More's Dialogue* (1531), Tyndale was done. For Thomas More, however, there were "close on three quarters of a million words against Tyndale . . . [compared to] Tyndale's eighty thousand in his *Answer.*" Ibid., p. 277.
[5]Ibid., p. 216.

offering my body to suffer what pain or torture, yea, what death his grace will, so this be obtained. Until that time, I will abide the asperity of all chances, whatsoever shall come, and endure my life in as many pains as it is able to bear and suffer.[6]

In other words, Tyndale would give himself up to the king on one condition—that the king authorize an English Bible translated from the Greek and Hebrew in the common language of the people.

The king refused. And Tyndale never went to his homeland again. Instead, if the king and the Roman Catholic Church would not provide a printed Bible in English for the common man to read, Tyndale would, even if it cost him his life—which it did five years later.

As I Live, the Plowboy Will Know His Bible

When he was twenty-eight years old in 1522, he was serving as a tutor in the home of John Walsh in Gloucestershire, England, spending most of his time studying Erasmus' Greek New Testament that had been printed just six years before in 1516.

We should pause here and make clear what an incendiary thing this Greek New Testament was in history. David Daniell describes the magnitude of this event:

This was the first time that the Greek New Testament had been printed. It is no exaggeration to say that it set fire to Europe. Luther [1483–1546] translated it into his famous

---

[6]Ibid.

German version of 1522. In a few years there appeared translations from the Greek into most European vernaculars. They
were the true basis of the popular reformation.[7]

Every day William Tyndale was seeing these Reformation
truths more clearly in the Greek New Testament as an ordained
Catholic priest. Increasingly, he was making himself suspect in
this Catholic house of John Walsh. Learned men would come for
dinner, and Tyndale would discuss the things he was seeing in the
New Testament. John Foxe tells us that one day an exasperated
Catholic scholar at dinner with Tyndale said, "We were better be
without God's law than the pope's."

In response Tyndale spoke his famous words, "I defy the
Pope and all his laws. . . . If God spare my life ere many years,
I will cause a boy that driveth the plow, shall know more of the
Scripture than thou dost."[8]

The One Note Crescendo

Four years later Tyndale finished the English translation of
the Greek New Testament in Worms, Germany, and began to
smuggle it into England in bales of cloth. He had grown up in
Gloucestershire, the cloth-working county, and now we see what

---

[7]William Tyndale, *Selected Writings*, edited with an introduction by David Daniell (New York:
Routledge, 2003), p. ix. "Modern champions of the Catholic position like to support a view
of the Reformation, that it was entirely a political imposition by a ruthless minority in power
against both the traditions and the wishes of the pious people of England. . . . The energy which
affected every human life in northern Europe, however, came from a different place. It was not
the result of political imposition. It came from the discovery of the Word of God as originally
written . . . in the language of the people. Moreover, it could be read and understood, without
censorship by the Church or mediation through the Church. . . . Such reading produced a
totally different view of everyday Christianity: the weekly, daily, even hourly ceremonies so
lovingly catalogued by some Catholic revisionists are not there; purgatory is not there; there is
no aural confession and penance. Two supports of the Church's wealth and power collapsed.
Instead there was simply individual faith in Christ the Saviour, found in Scripture. That and
only that 'justified' the sinner, whose root failings were now in the face of God, not the bishops
or the pope." Daniell, *Tyndale*, p. 58.
[8]Daniell, *Tyndale*, p. 79.

that turn of providence was about.[9] By October 1526, the book had been banned by Bishop Tunstall in London, but the print run had been at least three thousand. And the books were getting to the people. Over the next eight years, five pirated editions were printed as well.[10]

In 1534, Tyndale published a revised New Testament, having learned Hebrew in the meantime, probably in Germany, which helped him better understand the connections between the Old and New Testaments. Daniell calls this 1534 New Testament "the glory of his life's work."[11] If Tyndale was "always singing one note," this was the crescendo of the song of his life—the finished and refined New Testament in English.

The Very First New Testament in English from the Greek

For the first time ever in history, the Greek New Testament was translated into English. And for the first time ever, the New Testament in English was available in a printed form. Before Tyndale, there were only handwritten manuscripts of the Bible in English. These manuscripts we owe to the work and inspiration of John Wycliffe and the Lollards[12] from a hundred and thirty years earlier.[13] For a thousand years, the only translation of the Greek and Hebrew Bible was the Latin Vulgate, and few people could understand it, even if they had access to it.

---

[9]"Not for nothing did William Tyndale, exiled in Cologne, Worms and Antwerp use the international trade routes of the cloth merchants to get his books into England, smuggled in bales of cloth." Ibid., p. 15.
[10]Ibid., p. 188.
[11]Ibid., p. 316.
[12]"In the summer of 1382, Wyclif was attacked in a sermon preached at St. Mary's, Oxford, and his followers were for the first time denounced as 'Lollards'—a loose and suitably meaningless term of abuse ('mutterers') current in the Low Countries for Bible students, and thus heretics." David Daniell, *The Bible in English: Its History and Influence* (New Haven, CT: Yale University Press, 2003), p. 73.
[13]Gutenberg's printing press came in 1450.

Before he was martyred in 1536, Tyndale had translated into clear, common English[14] not only the New Testament[15] but also the Pentateuch, Joshua to 2 Chronicles, and Jonah.[16] All this material became the basis of the *Great Bible* issued by Miles Coverdale in England in 1539[17] and the basis for the *Geneva Bible* published in 1557—"the Bible of the nation,"[18] which sold over a million copies between 1560 and 1640.

Under God, Tyndale Gave Us Our English Bible

We do not get a clear sense of Tyndale's achievement without some comparisons. We think of the dominant King James Version as giving us the pervasive language of the English Bible. But Daniell clarifies the situation:

> William Tyndale gave us our English Bible. The sages assembled by King James to prepare the Authorized Version of 1611, so often praised for unlikely corporate inspiration, took over Tyndale's work. Nine-tenths of the Authorized Version's New Testament is Tyndale's. The same is true of the first half of the Old Testament, which was as far as he

[14] "Tyndale transmitted an English strength which is the opposite of Latin, seen in the difference between 'high' and 'elevated', 'gift' and 'donation', 'many' and 'multitudinous.'" Daniell, *Tyndale*, p. 3.
[15] Tyndale did not follow Luther in putting Hebrews, James, Jude, and Revelation in a special section of the New Testament set apart as inferior. "Tyndale, as shown later by his preface to James in his 1534 New Testament, is not only wiser and more generous—he is more true to the New Testament." Ibid., p. 120.
[16] This is available in print with all its original notes and introductions: *Tyndale's Old Testament*, trans. William Tyndale (New Haven, CT: Yale University Press, 1992). Also available is *Tyndale's New Testament*, trans. William Tyndale (New Haven, CT: Yale University Press, 1989).
[17] How could it be that Tyndale was martyred in 1536 for translating the Bible into English, and that his New Testament could be burned in London by Bishop Tunstall, and yet an entire printed Bible, essentially Tyndale's, *The Great Bible*, could be published in England three years later officially endorsed by this Bible-burning bishop? Daniell explains: "Tunstall, whose name would shortly appear on the title pages approving two editions of the Great Bible, was playing politics, being a puppet of the Pope through Wolsey and the king, betraying his Christian humanist learning at the direction of the church, needing to be receiving [Thomas] Wolsey's favor. . . . To burn God's word for politics was to Tyndale barbarous." Daniell, *Tyndale*, p. 93.
[18] Tyndale, *Selected Writings*, p. xi.

was able to get before he was executed outside Brussels in 1536.[19]

Here is a sampling of the English phrases we owe to Tyndale:

"Let there be light." (Genesis 1:3)

"Am I my brother's keeper?" (Genesis 4:9)

"The LORD bless thee and keep thee. The LORD make his face to shine upon thee and be merciful unto thee. The LORD lift up his countenance upon thee, and give thee peace." (Numbers 6:24–26)

"There were shepherds abiding in the field." (Luke 2:8)

"Blessed are they that mourn for they shall be comforted." (Matthew 5:4)

"Our Father, which art in heaven, hallowed be thy name." (Matthew 6:9)

"The signs of the times" (Matthew 16:3)

"The spirit is willing but the flesh is weak." (Matthew 26:41)

---

[19]*Tyndale*, p. 1. Daniell speaks with more precision elsewhere and says that the Authorized Version is 83 percent Tyndale's (Tyndale, *Selected Writings*, p. vii). Brian Moynahan, *God's Bestseller: William Tyndale, Thomas More, and the Writing of the English Bible—A Story of Martyrdom and Betrayal* (New York: St. Martin's Press, 2002), p. 1, confirms this with his estimates: Tyndale's words "account for 84 percent of the [King James Version] New Testament and 75.8 percent of the Old Testament books that he translated." Daniell also points out how remarkable the Old Testament translations were: "These opening chapters of Genesis are the first translations—not just the first printed, but the first translations—from Hebrew into English. This needs to be emphasized. Not only was the Hebrew language only known in England in 1529 and 1530 by, at the most, a tiny handful of scholars in Oxford and Cambridge, and quite possibly by none; that there was a language called Hebrew at all, or that it had any connection whatsoever with the Bible, would have been news to most of the ordinary population." *Tyndale*, p. 287.

"He went out . . . and wept bitterly." (Matthew 26:75)[20]

"In the beginning was the Word and the Word was with God and the Word was God." (John 1:1)

"In him we live, move and have our being." (Acts 17:28)

"A law unto themselves" (Romans 2:14)

"Though I speak with the tongues of men and of angels" (1 Corinthians 13:1)

"Fight the good fight." (1 Timothy 6:12)

According to Daniell, "The list of such near-proverbial phrases is endless."[21] Five hundred years after his great work, "newspaper headlines still quote Tyndale, though unknowingly, and he has reached more people than even Shakespeare."[22]

He Gave Us New Prose—and a Reformation

Luther's translation of 1522 is often praised for "having given a language to the emerging German nation." Daniell claims the same for Tyndale in English:

> In his Bible translations, Tyndale's conscious use of every-day words, without inversions, in a neutral word-order, and his wonderful ear for rhythmic patterns, gave to English not only a Bible language, but a new prose. England was blessed as a nation in that the language of its principal book, as

---

[20]"Wept bitterly" is still used by almost all modern translations (NIV, NASB, ESV, NKJV). It has not been improved on for five hundred years in spite of weak efforts like one recent translation: "cried hard." Unlike that phrase, "the rhythm of his two words carries the experience." Tyndale, *Selected Writings*, p. xv.
[21]Daniell, *Tyndale*, p. 142.
[22]Ibid., p. 2.

the Bible in English rapidly became, was the fountain from which flowed the lucidity, suppleness and expressive range of the greatest prose thereafter.[23]

His craftsmanship with the English language amounted to genius.[24]

He translated two-thirds of the Bible so well that his translations endured until today.[25]

This was not merely a literary phenomenon; it was a spiritual explosion. Tyndale's Bible and writings were the kindling that set the Reformation on fire in England.

Two Ways to Die to Bear Fruit for God

The question arises: How did William Tyndale accomplish this historic achievement? We can answer this in Tyndale's case by remembering two ways that a pastor or any spiritual leader must die in order to bear fruit for God (John 12:24; Romans 7:4). On the one hand, we must die to the notion that we do not have to think hard or work hard to achieve spiritual goals. On the other hand, we must die to the notion that our thinking and our working is decisive in achieving spiritual goals.

Paul said in 2 Timothy 2:7, "Think over what I say, for the Lord will give you understanding in everything." First, think. Work. Don't bypass the hard work of thinking about apostolic truth. But second, remember this: "*The Lord* will give

---

[23]Ibid., p. 116.
[24]Tyndale, *Selected Writings*, p. xv.
[25]Daniell, *Tyndale*, p. 121. "Tyndale gave the nation a Bible language that was English in words, word-order and lilt. He invented some words (for example, 'scapegoat') and the great Oxford English Dictionary has mis-attributed, and thus also mis-dated a number of his first uses." Ibid., p. 3.

you understanding." You work. He gives. If he withholds, all our working is in vain. But he ordains that we use our minds and that we work in achieving spiritual ends. So Paul says in 1 Corinthians 15:10, "I worked harder than any of them, though it was not I, but the grace of God that is with me." The key to spiritual achievement is to work hard, and to know and believe and be happy that God's sovereign grace is the decisive cause of all the good that comes.

How Erasmus and Tyndale Were Alike

The way these two truths come together in Tyndale's life explains how he could accomplish what he did. And one of the best ways to see it is to compare him with Erasmus, the Roman Catholic humanist scholar who was famous for his books *Enchiridion* and *The Praise of Folly* and for his printed Greek New Testament.

Erasmus was twenty-eight years older than Tyndale, but they both died in 1536—Tyndale martyred by the Roman Catholic Church, Erasmus a respected member of that church. Erasmus had spent time in Oxford and Cambridge, but we don't know if he and Tyndale ever met.

On the surface, one sees remarkable similarities between Tyndale and Erasmus. Both were great linguists. Erasmus was a Latin scholar and produced the first printed Greek New Testament. Tyndale knew eight languages: Latin, Greek, German, French, Hebrew, Spanish, Italian, and English. Both men loved the natural power of language and were part of a rebirth of interest in the way language works.

For example, Erasmus wrote a book called *De copia* that

Tyndale no doubt used as a student at Oxford.[26] It helped students increase their abilities to exploit the "copious" potential of language. This was hugely influential in the early 1500s in England and was used to train students in the infinite possibilities of varied verbal expression. The aim was to keep language from sinking down to mere jargon and worn-out slang and uncreative, unimaginative, prosaic, colorless, boring speech.

One practice lesson for students from *De copia* was to give "no fewer than one hundred fifty ways of saying 'Your letter has delighted me very much.'" The point was to force students to "use of all the verbal muscles in order to avoid any hint of flabbiness."[27] It is not surprising that this is the kind of educational world that gave rise to William Shakespeare (who was born in 1564). Shakespeare is renowned for his unparalleled use of copiousness in language. One critic wrote, "Without Erasmus, no Shakespeare."[28]

So both Erasmus and Tyndale were educated in an atmosphere of conscious craftsmanship.[29] That is, they both believed in hard work to say things clearly and creatively and compellingly when they spoke for Christ.

Not only that, but they both believed the Bible should be translated into the vernacular of every language. Erasmus wrote in the preface to his Greek New Testament,

> Christ wishes his mysteries to be published as widely as possible. I would wish even all women to read the gospel and the epistles of St. Paul, and I wish that they were translated

---

[26]"Tyndale could hardly have missed *De copia*." Daniell, *Tyndale*, p. 43. This book went through 150 additions by 1572.
[27]Ibid., p. 42.
[28]Emrys Jones, *The Origins of Shakespeare* (New York: Oxford University Press, 1977), p. 13.
[29]"Tyndale as conscious craftsman has been not just neglected, but denied: yet the evidence of the book that follows makes it beyond challenge that he used, as a master, the skill in the selection and arrangement of words which he partly learned at school and university, and partly developed from pioneering work by Erasmus." Daniell, *Tyndale*, p. 2.

into all languages of all Christian people, that they might be read and known, not merely by the Scotch and the Irish, but even by the Turks and the Saracens. I wish that the husbandman may sing parts of them at his plow, that the weaver may warble them at his shuttle, that the traveler may with their narratives beguile the weariness of the way.[30]

Tyndale could not have said it better.

Both were concerned with the corruption and abuses in the Catholic Church, and both wrote about Christ and the Christian life. Tyndale even translated Erasmus' *Enchiridion*, a kind of spiritual handbook for the Christian life—what Erasmus called *philosophia Christi*.

From a Lightning Bug to a Lightning Bolt

But there was a massive difference between these men, and it had directly to do with the other half of the paradox mentioned above, namely, that we must die not just to intellectual and linguistic laziness, but also to human presumption—human self-exaltation and self-sufficiency. Erasmus and Luther had clashed in the 1520s over the freedom of the will—Erasmus defending human self-determination and Luther arguing for the depravity and bondage of the will.[31] Tyndale was firmly with Luther here.

> Our will is locked and knit faster under the will of the devil than could an hundred thousand chains bind a man unto a post.[32]

---

[30]Ibid., p. 67.
[31]Erasmus' book was titled *On the Freedom of the Will,* and Luther's was *The Bondage of the Will.*
[32]Tyndale, *Selected Writings*, p. 39.

> Because . . . [by] nature we are evil, therefore we both think
> and do evil, and are under vengeance under the law, convict
> to eternal damnation by the law, and are contrary to the will
> of God in all our will and in all things consent to the will
> of the fiend.[33]

> It is not possible for a natural man to consent to the law,
> that it should be good, or that God should be righteous
> which maketh the law.[34]

This view of human sinfulness set the stage for Tyndale's grasp of
the glory of God's sovereign grace in the gospel. Erasmus—and
Thomas More with him—did not see the depth of the human
condition (their own condition) and so did not see the glory
and explosive power of what the reformers saw in the New
Testament. What the reformers like Tyndale and Luther saw was
not a *philosophia Christi* but the massive work of God in the
death and resurrection of Christ to save hopelessly enslaved and
hell-bound sinners.

Erasmus does not live or write in this realm of horrible condition and gracious blood-bought salvation. He has the appear-
ance of reform in the *Enchiridion*, but something is missing. To
walk from Erasmus into Tyndale is to move (to paraphrase Mark
Twain) from a lightning bug to a lightning bolt.

Daniell puts it like this:

> Something in the *Enchiridion* is missing. . . . It is a master-
> piece of humanist piety. . . . [But] the activity of Christ
> in the Gospels, his special work of salvation so strongly
> detailed there and in the epistles of Paul, is largely missing.
> Christologically, where Luther thunders, Erasmus makes a

---

[33]Ibid., p. 37.
[34]Ibid., p. 40.

sweet sound: what to Tyndale was an impregnable strong-
hold feels in the *Enchiridion* like a summer pavilion.[35]

Where Luther and Tyndale were blood-earnest about our dread-
ful human condition and the glory of salvation in Christ, Erasmus
and Thomas More joked and bantered. When Luther published
his Ninety-Five Theses in 1517, Erasmus sent a copy of them
to More—along with a "jocular letter including the anti-papal
games, and witty satirical diatribes against abuses within the
church, which both of them loved to make."[36]

The Difference: Clarity and Seriousness about the Gospel

I linger here with this difference between Tyndale and Erasmus
because I am trying to penetrate to how Tyndale accomplished
what he did through translating the New Testament. Explosive
reformation is what he accomplished in England. This was not
the effect of Erasmus' highbrow, elitist, layered nuancing of
Christ and church tradition. Erasmus and Thomas More may
have satirized the monasteries and clerical abuses, but they were
always playing games compared to Tyndale.

And in this they were very much like notable Christian writers in our own day. Listen to this remarkable assessment from
Daniell, and see if you do not hear a description of certain writers in our day who belittle doctrine and extol ambiguity as the
humble and mature mind-set:

Not only is there no fully realized Christ or Devil in
Erasmus's book . . . there is a touch of irony about it all,

---

[35]Daniell, *Tyndale*, pp. 68–69.
[36]Ibid., p. 254.

with a feeling of the writer cultivating a faintly superior ambiguity: as if to be dogmatic, for example about the full theology of the work of Christ, was to be rather distasteful, below the best, elite, humanist heights. . . . By contrast Tyndale . . . is ferociously single-minded ["always singing one note"]; the matter in hand, the immediate access of the soul to God without intermediary, is far too important for hints of faintly ironic superiority. . . . Tyndale is as foursquare as a carpenter's tool. But in Erasmus's account of the origins of his book there is a touch of the sort of layering of ironies found in the games with *personae*.[37]

It is ironic and sad that today supposedly avant-garde Christian writers can strike this cool, evasive, imprecise, artistic, superficially reformist pose of Erasmus and call it "*post*modern" and capture a generation of unwitting, historically naive people who don't know they are being duped by the same old verbal tactics used by the elitist, humanist writers in past generations. We see them in the controversies between the slippery Arians and Athanasius,[38] and we see them now in Tyndale's day. It's not postmodern. It's pre-modern—because it's perpetual.

At Root: A Passion for Justification by Faith

What drove Tyndale to sing "one note" all his life was the rock-solid conviction that all humans were in bondage to sin, blind, dead, damned, and helpless, and that God had acted in Christ to provide salvation by grace through faith. This is what lay hidden in the Latin Scriptures and the church system of penance and

---

[37]Ibid., pp. 69–70.
[38]See, for example, John Piper, *Contending for Our All: Defending the Truth and Treasuring Christ in the Lives of Athanasius, John Owen, and J. Gresham Machen* (Wheaton, IL: Crossway Books, 2006), p. 45.

merit. The Bible must be translated for the sake of the liberating,
life-giving gospel.[39]

There is only one hope for our liberation from the bonds of
sin and eternal condemnation, Tyndale said: "Neither can any
creature loose the bonds, save the blood of Christ only."[40]

> By grace . . . we are plucked out of Adam the ground of all evil
> and graffed [sic] in Christ, the root of all goodness. In Christ
> God loved us, his elect and chosen, before the world began
> and reserved us unto the knowledge of his Son and of his holy
> gospel:[41] and when the gospel is preached to us [it] openeth
> our hearts and giveth us grace to believe, and putteth the spirit
> of Christ in us: and we know him as our Father most merciful,
> and consent to the law and love it inwardly in our heart and
> desire to fulfill it and sorrow because we do not.[42]

This massive dose of bondage to sin and deliverance by blood-
bought sovereign grace[43] is missing in Erasmus. This is why there
is an elitist lightness to his religion—just like there is to so much
of evangelicalism today. Hell and sin and atonement and sovereign
grace were not weighty realities for Erasmus. But for Tyndale they

---

[39]"Central to Tyndale's insistence on the need for the Scriptures in English was his grasp that
Paul had to be understood in relation to each reader's salvation, and he needed there, above
all, to be clear." Daniell, *Tyndale*, p. 139.

[40]Tyndale, *Selected Writings*, p. 40.

[41]Here is Tyndale's definition of the "gospel" that rings with exuberant joy: "*Evangelion* (that
we call the gospel) is a Greek word and signifieth good, merry, glad and joyful tidings, that
maketh a man's heart glad and maketh him sing, dance, and leap for joy. . . . [This gospel is]
all of Christ the right David, how that he hath fought with sin, with death, and the devil, and
overcome them: whereby all men that were in bondage to sin, wounded with death, overcome
of the devil are without their own merits or deservings loosed, justified, restored to life and
saved, brought to liberty and reconciled unto the favor of God and set at one with him again:
which tidings as many as believe laud, praise and thank God, are glad, sing and dance for joy."
Ibid., p. 33.

[42]Ibid., p. 37.

[43]"Tyndale was more than a mildly theological thinker. He is at last being understood as,
theologically as well as linguistically, well ahead of his time. For him, as several decades later
for Calvin (and in the 20th century Karl Barth) the overriding message of the New Testament
is the sovereignty of God. Everything is contained in that. It must never, as he wrote, be lost
from sight. . . . Tyndale, we are now being shown, was original and new—except that he was
also old, demonstrating the understanding of God as revealed in the whole New Testament.
For Tyndale, God is, above all, sovereign, active in the individual and in history. He is the one
as he put it, in whom alone is found salvation and flourishing." Ibid., pp. viii-ix.

were everything. And in the middle of these great realities was the doctrine of justification by faith alone. This is why the Bible had to be translated, and ultimately this is why Tyndale was martyred.

> By faith are we saved only in believing the promises. And though faith be never without love and good works, yet is our saving imputed neither to love nor unto good works but unto faith only.[44]

> Faith the mother of all good works justifieth us, before we can bring forth any good work: as the husband marryeth his wife before he can have any lawful children by her.[45]

This is the answer to how William Tyndale accomplished what he did in translating the New Testament and writing books that set England on fire with the Reformed faith. He worked assiduously, like the most skilled artist, in the craft of compelling translation, and he was deeply passionate about the great doctrinal truths of the gospel of sovereign grace.

Man is lost, spiritually dead, condemned. God is sovereign; Christ is sufficient. Faith is all. Bible translation and Bible truth were inseparable for Tyndale, and in the end it was the truth—especially the truth of justification by faith alone—that ignited Britain with Reformed fire and then brought the death sentence to this Bible translator.

Blood-Serious Opposition to Bible Translation

It is almost incomprehensible to us today how viciously the Roman Catholic Church opposed the translation of the Scriptures

---

[44]Ibid., p. 38.
[45]Daniell, *Tyndale*, pp. 156–157.

into English. John Wycliffe and his followers called "Lollards"[46] had spread written manuscripts of English translations from the Latin in the late 1300s. In 1401, Parliament passed the law *de Haeretico Comburendo*—"on the burning of heretics"—to make heresy punishable by burning people alive at the stake. The Bible translators were in view.

Then in 1408, the Archbishop of Canterbury, Thomas Arundell, created the *Constitutions of Oxford*, which said,

> It is a dangerous thing, as witnesseth blessed St. Jerome, to translate the text of the Holy Scripture out of one tongue into another, for in the translation the same sense is not always easily kept. . . . We therefore decree and ordain, that no man, hereafter, by his own authority translate any text of the Scripture into English or any other tongue . . . and that no man can read any such book . . . in part or in whole.[47]

Together these statutes meant that you could be burned alive by the Catholic Church for simply reading the Bible in English. Let that sink in. The dramatist John Bale (1495–1563) "as a boy of 11 watched the burning of a young man in Norwich for possessing the Lord's prayer in English. . . . John Foxe records . . . seven Lollards burned at Coventry in 1519 for teaching their children the Lord's Prayer in English."[48]

The Burning Fury of More

Tyndale hoped to escape this condemnation by getting official authorization for his translation in 1524. But he found just the

---

[46]See note 12.
[47]Moynahan, *God's Bestseller*, p. xxii.
[48]William Tyndale, *The Obedience of A Christian Man*, edited with an introduction by David Daniell (London: Penguin Books, 2000), p. 202.

opposite and had to escape from London to the European continent where he did all his translating and writing for the next twelve years. He lived as a fugitive the entire time until his death near Brussels in 1536.

He watched a rising tide of persecution and felt the pain of seeing young men burned alive who were converted by reading his translation and his books. His closest friend, John Frith, was arrested in London and tried by Thomas More and burned alive July 4, 1531, at the age of twenty-eight. Richard Bayfield ran the ships that took Tyndale's books to England. He was betrayed and arrested, and Thomas More wrote on December 4, 1531, that Bayfield "the monk and apostate [was] well and worthily burned in Smythfelde."[49]

Three weeks later, the same end came to John Tewkesbury. He was converted by reading Tyndale's *Parable of the Wicked Mammon*, which defended justification by faith alone. He was whipped in Thomas More's garden and had his brow squeezed with small ropes until blood came out of his eyes. Then he was sent to the Tower where he was racked till he was lame. Then at last they burned him alive. Thomas More "rejoiced that his victim was now in hell, where Tyndale 'is like to find him when they come together.'"[50]

Four months later, James Bainham followed in the flames in April 1532. He had stood up during the mass at St. Augustine's Church in London and lifted a copy of Tyndale's New Testament and pleaded with the people to die rather than deny the word of God. That virtually was to sign his own death warrant. Add to these Thomas Bilney, Thomas Dusgate, John Bent, Thomas

---

[49]Moynahan, *God's Bestseller*, p. 260.
[50]Ibid., p. 261.

Harding, Andrew Hewet, Elizabeth Barton, and others, all burned alive for sharing the views of William Tyndale about the Scriptures and the Reformed faith.[51]

Why So Much Hatred?

Why this extraordinary hostility against the English New Testament, especially from Thomas More who vilified Tyndale repeatedly in his denunciation of the Reformers he burned? Some would say that the New Testament in English was rejected because it was accompanied with Reformation notes that the church regarded as heretical. That was true of later versions, but not of the first 1526 edition. It did not have notes, and this is the edition that Bishop Tunstall burned in London.[52] The church burned the word of God. They burned the Bible in public. That shocked Tyndale.

There were surface reasons and deeper reasons why the church opposed an English Bible. The surface reasons were the claims that the English language is rude and unworthy of the exalted language of God's word; and when one translates, errors can creep in, so it is safer not to translate. Moreover, if the Bible is in English, then each man will become his own interpreter, and many will go astray into heresy and be condemned; and it was church tradition that only priests are given the divine grace to understand the Scriptures. What's more, there is a special sacramental value to the Latin service that people cannot understand but through which grace is given. Such were the kinds of things being said on the surface.

---

[51]The list and details are given in Daniell, *Tyndale*, pp. 183–184.
[52]Ibid., pp. 192–193.

But there were deeper reasons why the church opposed the English Bible: one doctrinal (justification, which we will see in the last months of Tyndale's life) and the other ecclesiastical (the papal, sacramental structure of the Roman Catholic Church). The church realized that they would not be able to sustain certain doctrines biblically because the people would see that they are not in the Bible. And the church realized that their power and control over the people, and even over the state, would be lost if certain doctrines were exposed as unbiblical—especially the priesthood and purgatory and penance.

The Bible Must Not Be Available for Interpretation

Thomas More's criticism of Tyndale boils down mainly to the way Tyndale translated five words. He translated *presbuteros* as *elder* instead of *priest*. He translated *ekklesia* as *congregation* instead of *church*. He translated *metanoeo* as *repent* instead of *do penance*. He translated *exomologeo* as *acknowledge* or *admit* instead of *confess*. And he translated *agape* as *love* rather than *charity*.

Daniell comments, "He cannot possibly have been unaware that those words in particular undercut the entire sacramental structure of the thousand year church throughout Europe, Asia and North Africa. It was the Greek New Testament that was doing the undercutting."[53] And with the doctrinal undermining of these ecclesiastical pillars of priesthood and penance and confession, the pervasive power and control of the church collapsed. England would not be a Catholic nation. The Reformed faith would flourish there in due time.

---

[53]Ibid., p. 149.

The Sorrows and Sufferings of a Young Fugitive

What did it cost William Tyndale under these hostile circumstances to stay faithful to his calling as a translator of the Bible and a writer of the Reformed faith?

He fled his homeland in 1524 and was burned at the stake in 1536. He gives us some glimpse of those twelve years as a fugitive in Germany and the Netherlands in one of the very few personal descriptions we have, from Stephen Vaughan's letter in 1531. He refers to

> . . . my pains . . . my poverty . . . my exile out of mine natural country, and bitter absence from my friends . . . my hunger, my thirst, my cold, the great danger wherewith I am everywhere encompassed, and finally . . . innumerable other hard and sharp fightings which I endure.[54]

All these sufferings came to a climax on May 21, 1535, in the midst of Tyndale's great Old Testament translation labors. We can feel some of the ugliness of what happened in the words of David Daniell: "Malice, self-pity, villainy and deceit were about to destroy everything. These evils came to the English House [in Antwerp], wholly uninvited, in the form of an egregious Englishman, Henry Philips."[55] Philips had won Tyndale's trust over some months and then betrayed him. John Foxe tells how it happened:

> So when it was dinner-time, Master Tyndale went forth with Philips, and at the going forth of Poyntz's house, was a long narrow entry, so that two could not go in a front. Mr. Tyndale would have put Philips before him, but Philips

---

[54]Ibid., p. 213.
[55]Ibid., p. 361.

would in no wise, but put Master Tyndale before, for that he pretended to show great humanity. So Master Tyndale, being a man of no great stature, went before, and Philips, a tall comely person, followed behind him: who had set officers on either side of the door upon two seats, who, being there, might see who came in the entry: and coming through the same entry, Philips pointed with his finger over Master Tyndale's head down to him, that the officers who sat at the door might see that it was he whom they should take. . . . Then they took him, and brought him to the emperor's attorney, or procurer-general, where he dined. Then came the procurer-general to the house of Poyntz, and sent away all that was there of Master Tyndale's, as well his books as other things: and from thence Tyndale was had to the castle of Filford, eighteen English miles from Antwerp, and there he remained until he was put to death.[56]

The Cold and Final Castle

Vilvorde Castle is six miles north of Brussels and about the same distance from Louvain. Here Tyndale stayed for eighteen months. "The charge was heresy, with not agreeing with the holy Roman Emperor—in a nutshell, being Lutheran."[57] A four-man commission from the Catholic center of Louvain was authorized to prove that Tyndale was a heretic. One of them named Latomus filled three books with his interactions with Tyndale and said that Tyndale himself wrote a "book" in prison to defend his chief doctrinal standard: *Sola fides justificat apud Deum—Faith Alone Justifies Before God*. This was the key issue in the end. The evil of translating the Bible came down to this: Are we justified by faith alone?

[56]Ibid., p. 364.
[57]Ibid., p. 365.

These months in prison were not easy. They were a long dying, leading to death. We get one glimpse into the prison to see Tyndale's condition and his passion. He wrote a letter in September 1535, when there seems to have been a lull in the examinations. It was addressed to an unnamed officer of the castle. Here is a condensed version of Mozley's translation of the Latin:

> I beg your lordship, and that of the Lord Jesus, that if I am to remain here through the winter, you will request the commissary to have the kindness to send me, from the goods of mine which he has, a warmer cap; for I suffer greatly from cold in the head, and am afflicted by a perpetual catarrh, which is much increased in this cell; a warmer coat also, for this which I have is very thin; a piece of cloth too to patch my leggings. My overcoat is worn out; my shirts are also worn out. He has a woolen shirt, if he will be good enough to send it. I have also with him leggings of thicker cloth to put on above; he has also warmer night-caps. And I ask to be allowed to have a lamp in the evening; it is indeed wearisome sitting alone in the dark. But most of all I beg and beseech your clemency to be urgent with the commissary, that he will kindly permit me to have the Hebrew Bible, Hebrew grammar, and Hebrew dictionary, that I may pass the time in that study. In return may you obtain what you most desire, so only that it be for the salvation of your soul. But if any other decision has been taken concerning me, to be carried out before winter, I will be patient, abiding the will of God, to the glory of the grace of my Lord Jesus Christ: whose spirit (I pray) may ever direct your heart. Amen W. Tindalus[58]

We don't know if his requests were granted. He did stay in that prison through the winter. His verdict was sealed in August 1536. He was formally condemned as a heretic and degraded from the

---

[58]Ibid., p. 379.

priesthood. Then in early October (traditionally October 6), he was tied to the stake and then strangled by the executioner, then afterward consumed in the fire. Foxe reports that his last words were, "Lord! Open the King of England's eyes!"[59] He was forty-two years old, never married, and never buried.

He Will Ease Your Pain or Shorten It

His closing words to us are clear from his life and from his writings. Following God's call in accomplishing the spread of his saving gospel is often very costly. I will let him speak in his own words from his book *The Obedience of a Christian Man*:

> If God promise riches, the way thereto is poverty. Whom he loveth he chasteneth, whom he exalteth, he casteth down, whom he saveth he damneth first, he bringeth no man to heaven except he send him to hell first. If he promise life he slayeth it first, when he buildeth, he casteth all down first. He is no patcher, he cannot build on another man's foundation. He will not work until all be past remedy and brought unto such a case, that men may see how that his hand, his power, his mercy, his goodness and truth hath wrought all together. He will let no man be partaker with him of his praise and glory.[60]

> Let us therefore look diligently whereunto we are called, that we deceive not ourselves. We are called, not to dispute as the pope's disciples do, but to die with Christ that we may live with him, and to suffer with him that we may reign with him.[61]

---

[59]Ibid., pp. 382–383. "Contemporaries noted no such words, however, only that the strangling was bungled and that he suffered terribly." Moynahan, *God's Bestseller*, p. 377.
[60]Tyndale, *The Obedience of a Christian Man*, p. 6.
[61]Ibid., p. 8.

For if God be on our side: what matter maketh it who be against us, be they bishops, cardinals, popes or whatsoever names they will.[62]

So let Tyndale's very last word to us be the last word he sent to his best friend, John Frith, in a letter just before Frith was burned alive for believing and speaking the truth of Scripture:

Your cause is Christ's gospel, a light that must be fed with the blood of faith. . . . If when we be buffeted for well-doing, we suffer patiently and endure, that is acceptable to God; for to that end we are called. For Christ also suffered for us, leaving us an example, that we should follow his steps, who did no sin.

Hereby have we perceived love, that he had lain down his life for us; therefore we ought also to lay down our lives for the brethren. . . . Let not your body faint. . . . If the pain be above your strength, remember, Whatsoever ye shall ask in my name, I will give it you. And pray to our Father in that name, and he will ease your pain, or shorten it. . . . Amen.[63]

---

[62]Ibid., p. 6.
[63]From *Foxe's Book of Martyrs*.

2

JOHN G. PATON

"You Will Be Eaten by Cannibals!":
Courage in the Face of Fierce Opposition

In 1606, a chain of eighty islands in the South Pacific was discovered by Fernandez de Quiros of Spain. In 1773, the islands were explored by Captain James Cook and named the New Hebrides because of the similarities with the Hebrides Islands off the northwest coast of Scotland. In 1980, the New Hebrides gained its independence from Britain and France and was named Vanuatu. The chain of islands is about 450 miles long. If you draw a line straight from Honolulu to Sydney, it will cut through Port Vila, the capital of Vanuatu, two-thirds of the way between Hawaii and Australia. The population today is about 215,000.

Baptized with the Blood of Martyrs

To the best of our knowledge, the New Hebrides had no Christian influence before John Williams and James Harris from the London Missionary Society landed in 1839. Both of these missionaries were killed and eaten by cannibals on the island of Erromanga on November 20 of that year, only minutes after going ashore. Forty-eight years later, John Paton wrote, "Thus were the New Hebrides baptized with the blood of martyrs; and

Christ thereby told the whole Christian world that he claimed these islands as His own."[1]

The London Missionary Society sent another team to the island of Tanna in 1842, and these missionaries were driven off within seven months. But on the island of Aneityum, John Geddie from the Presbyterian Church in Nova Scotia (coming in 1848) and John Inglis from the Reformed Presbyterian Church in Scotland (coming in 1852) saw amazing fruit, so that by 1854 "about 3,500 savages [more than half the population[2]] threw away their idols, renouncing their heathen customs and avowing themselves to be worshippers of the true Jehovah God."[3] When Geddie died in 1872, all the population of Aneityum was said to be Christian.[4]

The Dangerous and Hope-filled Setting of Paton's Mission

This is part of a great work God was doing in the South Sea Islands in those days. In 1887, the sixty-three-year-old John Paton recorded the wider triumphs of the gospel. When certain people argued that the Aborigines of Australia were subhuman and incapable of conversion or civilization, Paton responded with mission facts as well as biblical truth.

> Recall . . . what the Gospel has done for the near kindred of these same Aborigines. On our own Aneityum, 3,500 Cannibals have been lead to renounce their heathenism. . . . In Fiji, 79,000 Cannibals have been brought under the influ-

---

[1]John G. Paton, *Missionary to the New Hebrides: An Autobiography Edited by His Brother* (1889, 1891; reprint, Edinburgh: The Banner of Truth, 1965), p. 75.
[2]Kenneth Scott Latourette, *A History of the Expansion of Christianity, The Great Century: The Americas, Australasia and Africa, 1800 AD to 1914 AD* (1943; reprint, Grand Rapids, MI: Zondervan, 1970), p. 228.
[3]*Autobiography*, p. 77.
[4]George Patterson, *Missionary Life among the Cannibals: Being the Life of the Rev. John Geddie, D.D., First Missionary to the New Hebrides; with the History of the Nova Scotia Presbyterian Mission on That Group* (Toronto: James Campbell and Son, 1882), p. 508.

ence of the Gospel; and 13,000 members of the Churches are professing to live and work for Jesus. In Samoa, 34,000 Cannibals have professed Christianity; and in nineteen years, its College has sent forth 206 Native teachers and evangelists. On our New Hebrides, more than 12,000 Cannibals have been brought to sit at the feet of Christ, though I mean not to say that they are all model Christians; and 133 of the Natives have been trained and sent forth as teachers and preachers of the Gospel.[5]

This is the remarkable missionary context for the life and ministry of John G. Paton, who was born near Dumfries, Scotland, on May 24, 1824. He sailed for the New Hebrides (via Australia) with his wife Mary on April 16, 1858, at the age of thirty-three. They reached their appointed island of Tanna on November 5, and in March the next year both his wife and his newborn son died of the fever. He served alone on the island for the next four years under incredible circumstances of constant danger until he was driven off the island in February 1862.

For the next four years, he did extraordinarily effective mobilization work for the Presbyterian mission to the New Hebrides, traveling around Australia and Great Britain. He married again in 1864 and took his wife Margaret back this time to the smaller island of Aniwa ("It measures scarcely seven miles by two"[6]). They labored together for forty-one years until Margaret died in 1905 when John Paton was eighty-one.

When they came to Aniwa in November 1866, they saw the destitution of the islanders. It will help us appreciate the magnitude of their labors and the wonders of their fruitfulness if we see some of what they faced.

---

[5]*Autobiography*, p. 265.
[6]Ibid., p. 312.

The native people were cannibals and occasionally ate the flesh of their defeated foes. They practiced infanticide and widow sacrifice, killing the widows of deceased men so they could serve their husbands in the next world.[7]

> Their worship was entirely a service of fear, its aim being to propitiate this or that evil spirit, to prevent calamity or to secure revenge. They deified their chiefs . . . so that almost every village or tribe had its own Sacred Man. . . . They exercised an extraordinary influence for evil, these village or tribal priests, and were believed to have the disposal of life and death through their sacred ceremonies. . . . They also worshipped the spirits of departed ancestors and heroes, through their material idols of wood and stone. . . . They feared the spirits and sought their aid; especially seeking to propitiate those who presided over war and peace, famine and plenty, health and sickness, destruction and prosperity, life and death. Their whole worship was one of slavish fear; and, so far as ever I could learn, they had no idea of a God of mercy or grace.[8]

Paton admitted that at times his heart wavered as he wondered whether these people could be brought to the point of weaving Christian ideas into the spiritual consciousness of their lives.[9] But he took heart from the power of the gospel and from the fact that thousands on Aneityum had come to Christ.

So he learned the language and reduced it to writing.[10] He built orphanages ("We trained these young people for Jesus"[11]). "Mrs. Paton taught a class of about fifty women and

---

[7]Ibid., pp. 69, 334.
[8]Ibid., p. 72. This description was made of the natives on the island of Tanna but applies equally well to the conditions on the nearby island of Aniwa.
[9]Ibid., p. 74.
[10]Ibid., p. 319.
[11]Ibid., p. 317.

girls. They became experts at sewing, singing and plaiting hats, and reading."[12] They "trained the Teachers . . . translated and printed and expounded the Scriptures . . . ministered to the sick and dying . . . dispensed medicines every day . . . taught them the use of tools . . ." and more.[13] They held worship services every Lord's Day and sent native teachers to all the villages to preach the gospel.

In the next fifteen years, John and Margaret Paton saw the entire island of Aniwa turn to Christ. Years later he wrote, "I claimed Aniwa for Jesus, and by the grace of God Aniwa now worships at the Savior's feet."[14] When he was seventy-three years old and traveling around the world trumpeting the cause of missions in the South Seas, he was still ministering to his beloved Aniwan people and "published the New Testament in the Aniwan Language" in 1897.[15] Even to his death, he was translating hymns and catechisms[16] and creating a dictionary for his people even when he couldn't be with them anymore.[17]

During his years of labor on the islands, Paton kept a journal and notebooks and letters from which he wrote his *Autobiography* in three parts from 1887 to 1898. Almost all we know of his work comes from that book, which is still in print in one volume from the Banner of Truth Trust.

Paton outlived his wife by two years and died in Australia on January 28, 1907, at the age of eighty-two. Today, over a hundred years after the death of John Paton, about 91 percent of the population of Vanuatu identifies itself as Christian, perhaps 14

---

[12]Ibid., p. 377.
[13]Ibid., p. 378.
[14]Ibid., p. 312.
[15]Ralph Bell, *John G. Paton: Missionary to the New Hebrides* (Butler, IN: The Highley Press, 1957), p. 238.
[16]Ibid.
[17]*Autobiography*, p. 451.

percent of the population being evangelical.[18] The sacrifices and the legacy of the missionaries to the New Hebrides are stunning, and John G. Paton stands out as one of the great ones. In telling his story, we will focus on one of the most inspiring aspects of his character: his courage.

Overcoming Criticism

Paton had courage to overcome the criticism he received from respected elders for going to the New Hebrides. A certain Mr. Dickson exploded, "The cannibals! You will be eaten by cannibals!" The memory of Williams and Harris on Erromanga was only nineteen years old. But to this Paton responded:

> Mr. Dickson, you are advanced in years now, and your own prospect is soon to be laid in the grave, there to be eaten by worms; I confess to you, that if I can but live and die serving and honoring the Lord Jesus, it will make no difference to me whether I am eaten by Cannibals or by worms; and in the Great Day my Resurrection body will rise as fair as yours in the likeness of our risen Redeemer.[19]

This is the kind of in-your-face spiritual moxie that would mark Paton's whole life. It's a big part of what makes reading his story so invigorating.

Another kind of criticism for his going was that he would be leaving a very fruitful ministry. Paton had served for ten years as a city missionary in urban Glasgow among lower-income people with tremendous success, and hundreds of unchurched

---

[18]See the Joshua Project, http://www.joshuaproject.net/peopctry.php?rop3=110511&rog3=NH; accessed 05-06-08.
[19]*Autobiography*, p. 56.

people were attending his classes and services during the week. One of his loved professors of divinity and minister of the congregation where he had served as an elder tried to persuade him to stay in that ministry. He reported that the professor made his case as follows:

> Green Street Church was doubtless the sphere for which God had given me peculiar qualifications, and in which He had so largely blessed my labors; that if I left those now attending my Classes and Meetings, they might be scattered, and many of them would probably fall away; that I was leaving certainty for uncertainty—work in which God had made me greatly useful, for work in which I might fail to be useful, and only throw away my life amongst Cannibals.[20]

Paton said the opposition to his going was deeply troubling:

> The opposition was so strong from nearly all, and many of them warm Christian friends, that I was sorely tempted to question whether I was carrying out the Divine will, or only some headstrong wish of my own. This also caused me much anxiety, and drove me close to God in prayer.[21]

We will see shortly how he rose above these temptations to turn away from his missionary calling.

Courage in the Face of Possible and Real Loss

He and his wife arrived on the island of Tanna on November 5, 1858, and Mary was pregnant. The baby was born February 12, 1859. "Our island-exile thrilled with joy! But the greatest of sor-

---

[20]Ibid., p. 55.
[21]Ibid., p. 56.

rows was treading hard upon the heels of that great joy!"[22] Mary had repeated attacks of ague, fever, pneumonia, and diarrhea with delirium for two weeks.

> Then in a moment, altogether unexpectedly, she died on March third. To crown my sorrows, and complete my loneliness, the dear baby-boy, whom we had named after her father, Peter Robert Robson, was taken from me after one week's sickness, on the 20th of March. Let those who have ever passed through any similar darkness as of midnight feel for me; as for all others, it would be more than vain to try to paint my sorrows![23]

He dug the two graves with his own hands and buried them by the house he had built.

> Stunned by that dreadful loss, in entering upon this field of labor to which the Lord had Himself so evidently led me, my reason seemed for a time almost to give way. The ever-merciful Lord sustained me . . . and that spot became my sacred and much-frequented shrine, during all the following months and years when I labored on for the salvation of the savage Islanders amidst difficulties, dangers, and deaths. . . . But for Jesus, and the fellowship he vouchsafed to me there, I must have gone mad and died beside the lonely grave![24]

The courage to risk the loss was remarkable. But the courage to experience the loss and press on alone was supernatural.

> I felt her loss beyond all conception or description, in that dark land. It was very difficult to be resigned, left alone, and in sorrowful circumstances; but feeling immovably assured

---

[22]Ibid., p. 79.
[23]Ibid.
[24]Ibid., p. 80.

that my God and father was too wise and loving to err in anything that He does or permits, I looked up to the Lord for help, and struggled on in His work.[25]

Here we get a glimpse of the theology that we will see underneath this man's massive courage and toil.

I do not pretend to see through the mystery of such visitations—wherein God calls away the young, the promising, and those sorely needed for his service here; but this I do know and feel, that, in the light of such dispensations, it becomes us all to love and serve our blessed Lord Jesus so that we may be ready at his call for death and eternity.[26]

Courage to Risk His Own Sickness with No Doctors and No Escape

"Fever and ague had attacked me fourteen times severely."[27] In view of his wife's death, he never knew when any one of these attacks would mean his own death. Imagine struggling with a life-and-death sickness over and over with only one Christian native friend named Abraham who had come with him to the island to help him.

For example, as he was building a new house to get to higher, healthier ground, he collapsed with the fever on his way up the steep hill from the coast:

When about two-thirds up the hill I became so faint that I concluded I was dying. Lying down on the ground, sloped against the root of a tree to keep me from rolling to the

---

[25]Ibid., p. 85.
[26]Ibid.
[27]Ibid., p. 105.

bottom, I took farewell of old Abraham, of my mission work, and of everything around! In this weak state I lay, watched over by my faithful companion, and fell into a quiet sleep.[28]

He revived and was restored. But only great courage could press on month after month, year after year, knowing that the fever that took his wife and son lay at the door.

And it's not as if these dangers were only during one season at the beginning of his missionary life. Fifteen years later with another wife and another child on another island, he records, "During the hurricanes, from January to April, 1873, when the *Dayspring* [the mission ship] was wrecked, we lost a darling child by death, my dear wife had a protracted illness, and I was brought very low with severe rheumatic fever . . . and was reported as dying."[29]

Courage to Face Mortal Enemies

The most common demand for courage was the almost constant threat to his life from the hostilities of the natives. This is what makes his *Autobiography* read like a thriller. In his first four years on Tanna, when he was all alone, he moved from one savage crisis to the next. One wonders how his mind kept from snapping, as he never knew when his house would be surrounded with angry natives or whether he would be ambushed along the way. How do you survive when there is no time or place for leisure? No unwinding? No sure refuge on earth?

---

[28]Ibid., p. 106.
[29]Ibid., p. 384.

Our continuous danger caused me now oftentimes to sleep
with my clothes on, that I might start at a moment's warn-
ing. My faithful dog Clutha would give a sharp bark and
awake me. . . . God made them fear this precious creature,
and often used her in saving our lives.[30]

My enemies seldom slackened their hateful designs against
my life, however calmed or baffled for the moment. . . .
A wild chief followed me around for four hours with
his loaded musket, and, though often directed towards
me, God restrained his hand. I spoke kindly to him, and
attended to my work as if he had not been there, fully
persuaded that my God had placed me there, and would
protect me till my allotted task was finished. Looking up
in unceasing prayer to our dear Lord Jesus, I left all in his
hands, and felt immortal till my work was done. Trials and
hairbreadth escapes strengthened my faith, and seemed only
to nerve me for more to follow; and they did tread swiftly
upon each other's heels.[31]

One of the most remarkable things about Paton's dealing with
danger is the gutsy forthrightness with which he spoke to his
assailants. He often rebuked them to their faces and scolded them
for their bad behavior even as they held the axe over his head.

One morning at daybreak I found my house surrounded by
armed men, and a chief intimated that they had assembled
to take my life. Seeing that I was entirely in their hands,
I knelt down and gave myself away body and soul to the
Lord Jesus, for what seemed the last time on earth. Rising,
I went out to them, and began calmly talking about their
unkind treatment of me and contrasting it with all my
conduct towards them. . . . At last some of the Chiefs, who

---

[30]Ibid., p. 178.
[31]Ibid., p. 117.

had attended the Worship, rose and said, "Our conduct has been bad; but now we will fight for you, and kill all those who hate you."[32]

[Once] when natives in large numbers were assembled at my house, a man furiously rushed on me with his axe but a Kaserumini Chief snatched a spade with which I had been working, and dexterously defended me from instant death. Life in such circumstances led me to cling very near to the Lord Jesus; I knew not, for one brief hour, when or how attack might be made; and yet, with my trembling hand clasped in the hand once nailed on Calvary, and now swaying the scepter of the universe, calmness and peace and resignation abode in my soul.[33]

As his courage increased and his deliverances were multiplied, he would make it his aim to keep warring factions separated, and he would throw himself between them and argue for peace. "Going amongst them every day, I did my utmost to stop hostilities, setting the evils of war before them, and pleading with the leading men to renounce it."[34] He would go to visit his enemies when they were sick and wanted his help, never knowing what was an ambush and what was not.

Once a native named Ian called Paton to his sickbed, and as Paton leaned over him, he pulled a dagger and held it to Paton's heart.

I durst neither move nor speak, except that my heart kept praying to the Lord to spare me, or if my time was come, to take me home to Glory with Himself. There passed a few moments of awful suspense. My sight went and came.

---

[32]Ibid., p. 115.
[33]Ibid., p. 117.
[34]Ibid., p. 139.

Not a word had been spoken, except to Jesus; and then Ian wheeled the knife around, thrust it into the sugar cane leaf. And [he] cried to me, "Go, go quickly!" . . . I ran for my life a weary four miles till I reached the Mission House, faint, yet praising God for such a deliverance.[35]

Courage to Die?

A final kind of courage I will mention is the courage in the face of accusations that he was a coward. After four years, the entire island population rose against Paton, blaming him for an epidemic, and made siege against him and his little band of Christians. There were spectacularly close calls and a miraculous deliverance from fire by wind and rain,[36] and finally a wonderful answer to prayer as a ship arrived just in time to take him off the island.

In response to this, and after four years of risking his life hundreds of times and losing his wife and child, he recounts,

> Conscious that I had, to the last inch of life, tried to do my duty, I left all results in the hands of my only Lord, and all criticisms to His unerring judgment. Hard things also were occasionally spoken to my face. One dear friend, for instance, said, "You should not have left. You should have stood at the post of duty till you fell. It would have been to your honor, and better for the cause of the Mission, had you been killed at the post of duty like the Gordons and others.[37]

Oh, how easy it would have been for him to respond by walking away from the mission at a moment like that. But courage pressed

---

[35]Ibid., p. 191.
[36]Ibid., p. 215.
[37]Ibid., p. 223.

on for another four decades of fruitful ministry on the island of Aniwa and around the world.

And so the next question I ask of Paton's life is, *What did this courage achieve?*

The Outcome of His Courage?

We have already seen one main answer to this question—namely, the entire island of Aniwa turned to Christ. Four years of seemingly fruitless and costly labor on Tanna could have meant the end of Paton's missionary life. He could have remembered that in Glasgow for ten years he had had unprecedented success as an urban missionary. Now for four years he seemed to have accomplished nothing, and he lost his wife and child in the process. But instead of going home, he turned his missionary heart to Aniwa. And this time the story was different. "I claimed Aniwa for Jesus, and by the grace of God, Aniwa now worships at the Savior's feet."[38]

Awakening at Home

The courageous endurance on Tanna resulted in a story that awakened thousands to the call of missions and strengthened the home church. The reason Paton wrote the second volume of his *Autobiography*, he says, was to record God's "marvelous goodness in using my humble voice and pen, and the story of my life, for interesting thousands and tens of thousands in the work of Missions."[39] And the influence goes on today—even, I pray, in this book.

[38]Ibid., p. 312.
[39]Ibid., p. 220.

Oftentimes, while passing through the perils and defeats of my first four years in the Mission-field on Tanna, I wondered . . . why God permitted such things. But on looking back now, I already clearly perceive . . . that the Lord was thereby preparing me for doing, and providing me materials where-with to accomplish, the best work of all my life, namely the kindling of the heart of Australian Presbyterianism with a living affection for these Islanders of their own Southern Seas . . . and in being the instrument under God of sending out Missionary after Missionary to the New Hebrides, to claim another island and still another for Jesus. That work, and all that may spring from it in Time and Eternity, never could have been accomplished by me but for first the suffer-ings and then the story of my Tanna enterprise![40]

And the awakening was not just in Australia, but in Scotland and around the world. For example, he tells us what the effect of his home tour was on his own small Reformed Presbyterian Church after his four years of pain and seeming fruitlessness on Tanna. "I was . . . filled with a high passion of gratitude to be able to proclaim, at the close of my tour . . . that of all her ordained Ministers, one in every six was a Missionary of the Cross!"[41] Indeed the effects at home were far more widespread than that, and here is a lesson for all churches today.

Nor did the dear old Church thus cripple herself; on the contrary, her zeal for Missions accompanied, if not caused, unwonted prosperity at home. New waves of liberality passed over the heart of her people. Debts that had burdened many of the Churches and Manses were swept away. Additional Congregations were organized. And in May, 1876, the Reformed Presbyterian Church entered into an honorable

---

[40]Ibid., pp. 222–223.
[41]Ibid., p. 280.

and independent Union with her larger, wealthier, and more progressive sister, the Free Church of Scotland.[42]

In other words, the courageous perseverance of John Paton on Tanna, in spite of apparent fruitlessness, bore fruit for the mission field and for the church at home in ways he could have never dreamed in the midst of his dangers.

Silencing Skeptics

Another one of those good effects was to vindicate the power of the gospel to convert the hardest people. Paton had an eye to the sophisticated European despisers of the gospel as he wrote the story of his life. He wanted to give evidence to skeptical modern men that the gospel can and does transform the most unlikely people and their societies.

So in his *Autobiography* he tells stories of particular converts like Kowia, a chief on Tanna. When he was dying, he came to say farewell to Paton.

> "Farewell, Missi, I am very near death now; we will meet again in Jesus and with Jesus!" . . . Abraham sustained him, tottering to the place of graves; there he lay down . . . and slept in Jesus; and there the faithful Abraham buried him beside his wife and children. Thus died a man who had been a cannibal chief, but by the grace of God and the love of Jesus changed, transfigured into a character of light and beauty. What think ye of this, ye skeptics as to the reality of conversion? . . . I knew that day, and I know now, that there is one soul at least from Tanna to sing the glories of Jesus in Heaven—and, oh, the rapture when I meet him there![43]

---

[42]Ibid.
[43]Ibid., p. 160.

And then, of course, there was old Abraham himself. He was not one of Paton's converts, but he was a converted cannibal from Aneityum and Paton's absolutely trustworthy helper on Tanna during all his time there. So Paton writes again as a witness to European skeptics:

> When I have read or heard the shallow objections of irreligious scribblers and talkers, hinting that there was no reality in conversions, and that mission effort was but waste, oh, how my heart has yearned to plant them just one week on Tanna, with the "natural" man all around in the person of Cannibal and Heathen, and only the one "spiritual" man in the person of the converted Abraham, nursing them, feeding them, saving them "for the love of Jesus"—that I might just learn how many hours it took to convince them that Christ in man was a reality after all! All the skepticism of Europe would hide its head in foolish shame; and all its doubts would dissolve under one glance of the new light that Jesus, and Jesus alone, pours from the converted Cannibal's eye.[44]

The list could go on as to what Paton's courage achieved. But we turn to the question, *Where did this courage come from?* But the two questions overlap, because what the courage achieved was the vindication of its source.

Where Did This Courage Come From?

The answer Paton would want us to give is that it came from God. But he would also want us to see what precious means God used and, if possible, apply them to ourselves and our situations.

---

[44]Ibid., p. 107.

What was it then that God used to awaken in John Paton such remarkable courage?

HIS COURAGE CAME FROM HIS FATHER

The tribute Paton pays to his godly father is worth the price of his *Autobiography*, even if you don't read anything else. Maybe it's because I have a daughter and four sons, but I wept as I read this section. It filled me with such longing to be a father like this.

There was a small room, the "closet" where his father would go for prayer, as a rule, after each meal. The eleven children knew it, and they reverenced the spot and learned something profound about God from their father's devotion to prayer. The impact on John Paton was immense.

> Though everything else in religion were by some unthinkable catastrophe to be swept out of memory, were blotted from my understanding, my soul would wander back to those early scenes, and shut itself up once again in that Sanctuary Closet, and, hearing still the echoes of those cries to God, would hurl back all doubt with the victorious appeal, "He walked with God, why may not I?"[45]

> How much my father's prayers at this time impressed me I can never explain, nor could any stranger understand. When, on his knees and all of us kneeling around him in Family Worship, he poured out his whole soul with tears for the conversion of the Heathen world to the service of Jesus, and for every personal and domestic need, we all felt as if in the presence of the living Savior, and learned to know and love him as our Divine friend.[46]

---

[45]Ibid., p. 8.
[46]Ibid., p. 21.

One scene best captures the depth of love between John and his father and the power of the impact on John's life of uncompromising courage and purity. The time came for the young Paton to leave home and go to Glasgow to attend divinity school and become a city missionary in his early twenties. From his hometown of Torthorwald to the train station at Kilmarnock was a forty-mile walk. Forty years later Paton wrote:

> My dear father walked with me the first six miles of the way. His counsels and tears and heavenly conversation on that parting journey are fresh in my heart as if it had been but yesterday; and tears are on my cheeks as freely now as then, whenever memory steals me away to the scene. For the last half mile or so we walked on together in almost unbroken silence—my father, as was often his custom, carrying hat in hand, while his long flowing yellow hair (then yellow, but in later years white as snow) streamed like a girl's down his shoulders. His lips kept moving in silent prayers for me; and his tears fell fast when our eyes met each other in looks for which all speech was vain! We halted on reaching the appointed parting place; he grasped my hand firmly for a minute in silence, and then solemnly and affectionately said: "God bless you, my son! Your father's God prosper you, and keep you from all evil!"
>
> Unable to say more, his lips kept moving in silent prayer; in tears we embraced, and parted. I ran off as fast as I could; and, when about to turn a corner in the road where he would lose sight of me, I looked back and saw him still standing with head uncovered where I had left him—gazing after me. Waving my hat in adieu, I rounded the corner and out of sight in an instant. But my heart was too full and sore to carry me further, so I darted into the side of the road and wept for a time. Then, rising up cautiously, I climbed the dike to see if he yet stood where I had left him;

and just at that moment I caught a glimpse of him climbing the dyke and looking out for me! He did not see me, and after he gazed eagerly in my direction for a while, he got down, set his face toward home, and began to return—his head still uncovered, and his heart, I felt sure, still rising in prayers for me. I watched through blinding tears, till his form faded from my gaze; and then, hastening on my way, vowed deeply and oft, by the help of God, to live and act so as never to grieve or dishonor such a father and mother as he had given me.[47]

The impact of his father's faith and prayer and love and discipline was immeasurable.

HIS COURAGE CAME FROM A DEEP SENSE OF DIVINE CALLING

Before he was twelve years old, Paton says, "I had given my soul to God, and was resolved to aim at being a missionary of the cross, or a minister of the gospel."[48] As he came to the end of his studies in divinity in Glasgow at the age of thirty-two, he says, "I continually heard . . . the wail of the perishing Heathen in the South Seas; and I saw that few were caring for them, while I well knew that many would be ready to take up my work in Calton."[49] "The Lord kept saying within me, 'Since none better qualified can be got, rise and offer yourself!'"

When he was criticized for leaving a fruitful ministry, one crucial event sealed his sense of calling, namely, a word from his parents:

---

[47]Ibid., pp. 25–26.
[48]Ibid. p. 21.
[49]Ibid., p. 52.

Heretofore we feared to bias you, but now we must tell you why we praise God for the decision to which you have been led. Your father's heart was set upon being a Minister, but other claims forced him to give it up. When you were given to them, your father and mother laid you upon the altar, their first-born, to be consecrated, if God saw fit, as a Missionary of the Cross; and it has been their constant prayer that you might be prepared, qualified, and led to this very decision; and we pray with all our heart that the Lord may accept your offering, long spare you, and give you many souls from the Heathen World for your hire.[50]

In response to that, Paton wrote, "From that moment, every doubt as to my path of duty forever vanished. I saw the hand of God very visibly, not only preparing me before, but now leading me to, the Foreign Mission field."[51] That sense of duty and calling bred in him an undaunted courage that would never look back.

His Courage Came from a Sense of Holy Heritage in His Church

Paton was part of the Reformed Presbyterian Church of Scotland, one of the oldest but smallest Protestant churches. It traced its lineage back to the Scottish Covenanters and had in it a strong sense of valor for the cause of the great truths of the Reformation. Paton once wrote, "I am more proud that the blood of Martyrs is in my veins, and their truths in my heart, than other men can be of noble pedigree or royal names."[52]

The truths he has in mind are the robust doctrines of Calvinism. He said in his *Autobiography*, "I am by conviction

---

[50]Ibid., p. 57.
[51]Ibid.
[52]Ibid., p. 280.

a strong Calvinist."[53] For him this meant, as we have seen, a strong confidence that God can and will change the hearts of the most unlikely people. His Reformed doctrine of regeneration was crucial here in maintaining his courage in the face of humanly impossible odds. Commenting on the conversion of one native, he said, "Regeneration is the sole work of the Holy Spirit in the human heart and soul, and is in every case one and the same. Conversion, on the other hand, bringing into play the action also of the human will, is never absolutely the same perhaps in even two souls."[54] "Oh, Jesus! To Thee alone be all the glory. Thou hast the key to unlock every heart that Thou has created."[55]

In other words, Calvinism, contrary to all misrepresentation, was not a hindrance to missions but the hope of missions for John Paton and hundreds of other missionaries like him. So it's not surprising what the next source of courage was for Paton.

His Courage Came from His Confidence in the Sovereignty of God Controlling All Adversities

We have already seen the words he wrote over his wife's and child's grave: "Feeling immovably assured that my God and father was too wise and loving to err in anything that he does or permits, I looked up to the Lord for help, and struggled on in His work."[56]

Over and over this faith sustained him in the most threatening and frightening situations. As he was trying to escape from Tanna at the end of four years of dangers, he and Abraham were surrounded by raging natives who kept urging each other to strike the first blow.

---

[53]Ibid., p. 195.
[54]Ibid., p. 372.
[55]Ibid., p. 373.
[56]Ibid., p. 85.

My heart rose up to the Lord Jesus; I saw Him watching all the scene. My peace came back to me like a wave from God. I realized that I was immortal till my Master's work with me was done. The assurance came to me, as if a voice out of Heaven had spoken, that not a musket would be fired to wound us, not a club prevail to strike us, not a spear leave the hand in which it was held vibrating to be thrown, not an arrow leave the bow, or a killing stone the fingers, without the permission of Jesus Christ, whose is all power in Heaven and on Earth. He rules all Nature, animate and inanimate, and restrains even the Savage of the South Seas.[57]

After getting away with his life and losing everything that he had on earth ("my little earthly All"), instead of despairing or pouting or being paralyzed with self-pity, he moved forward expecting to see God's good purpose in time—which he saw in the ministry that opened to him, first of missions mobilization and then of work on Aniwa. "Often since have I thought that the Lord stripped me thus bare of all these interests, that I might with undistracted mind devote my entire energy to the special work soon to be carved out for me, and of which at this moment neither I nor anyone had ever dreamed."[58]

Year after year, "disappointments and successes were strangely intermingled"[59] in his life. There was no long period of time, it seems, where life was very easy. But we would distort the man if we said there were no low moments. "I felt so disappointed, so miserable," he wrote about one period of his travels, "that I wished I had been in my grave with my dear departed and my brethren on the Islands who had fallen around me."[60] It was

[57]Ibid., p. 207.
[58]Ibid., p. 220.
[59]Ibid., p. 247.
[60]Ibid., p. 232.

not always easy after the words "The Lord has taken away" to add the words "Blessed be the name of the Lord." But the way out was clear, and he used it again and again. When the mission ship, *Dayspring*, that he had worked so hard to fund was sunk in a storm, he wrote:

> Whatever trials have befallen me in my Earthly Pilgrimage, I have never had the trial of doubting that perhaps, after all, Jesus had made some mistake. No! my blessed Lord Jesus makes no mistakes! When we see all His meaning, we shall then understand, what now we can only trustfully believe that all is well—best for us, best for the cause most dear to us, best for the good of others and the glory of God.[61]

Near the end of his life, at age seventy-nine, he was back on his beloved island Aniwa.

> I cannot visit the villages, or go among the people and the sick, as formerly, owing to an increased feebleness in my legs and lumbago. Which is painful for the last fortnight. But all is as our Master sends it, and we submit thankfully, as all is nothing to what we deserve; and adored be our God. We have in our dear Lord Jesus [grace] for peace and joy in all circumstances.[62]

HIS COURAGE CAME THROUGH A CERTAIN KIND OF PRAYING

The prayer that made all the difference was the kind that submitted to God's sovereign wisdom. How do you claim the promises

---

[61]Ibid., p. 488.
[62]Bell, *John G. Paton*, p. 238.

of God for protection when your wife was equally faithful but, rather than being protected, died? How do you bank on God's care when the Gordons on Erromanga were equally trusting in God's care and were martyred?[63] Paton had learned the answer to this question from listening to his mother pray, even before he learned the theology that supports it.

When the potato crop failed in Scotland, Mrs. Paton said to her children, "O my children, love your Heavenly Father, tell Him in faith and prayer all your needs, and He will supply your wants so far as it shall be for your good and His glory."[64] This is what Paton trusted God for in claiming the promises: God would supply all his needs insofar as this would be for Paton's good and for God's glory.

His courage, when he was surrounded by armed natives, came through a kind of praying that claimed the promises under the overarching submission to God's wisdom as to what would work most for God's glory and his good.

> I . . . assured them that I was not afraid to die, for at death my Savior would take me to be with Himself in Heaven, and to be far happier than I had ever been on Earth. I then lifted up my hands and eyes to the Heavens, and prayed aloud for

---

[63]Mr. and Mrs. G. N. Gordon were killed on Erromanga on May 20, 1861. They had labored four years on the island when they walked into an ambush.

"A blow was aimed at him with a tomahawk, which he caught; the other man struck, but his weapon was also caught. One of the tomahawks was then wrenched out of his grasp. Next moment, a blow on the spine laid the dear Missionary low, and a second on the neck almost severed the head from the body." Mrs. Gordon came running to see the noise and "Ouben slipped stealthily behind here, sank his tomahawk into her back and with another blow almost severed her head! This was the fate of those two devoted servants of the Lord; loving in their lives and in their deaths not divided, their spirits, wearing the crown of martyrdom, entered Glory together, to be welcomed by Williams and Harris, whose blood was shed near the same now hallowed spot for the name and the cause of Jesus." (*Autobiography*, p. 166)

[64]*Autobiography*, p. 22. Compare this way of praying with the way Shadrach, Meshach, and Abednego faced the fiery furnace in Daniel 3:17–18: "If this be so, our God whom we serve is able to deliver us from the burning fiery furnace, and he will deliver us out of your hand, O king. But if not, be it known to you, O king, that we will not serve your gods or worship the golden image that you have set up."

Jesus . . . either to protect me or to take me home to Glory
as He saw to be for the best.[65]

That was how he prayed again and again: "Protect me or . . .
take me home to Glory as you see to be for the best." He knew
that Jesus had promised suffering and martyrdom to some of his
servants (Luke 11:49; 21:12–18). So the promises he claimed
were both: either protect me, or take me home in a way that will
glorify you and do good for others.[66]

After one harrowing journey, he wrote, "Had it not been for the
assurance that . . . in every path of duty He would carry me through
or dispose of me therein for His glory, I could never have undertaken
either journey."[67] The peace God gave him in these crises was not
the peace of sure escape but the peace that God is good and wise and
omnipotent and will do all things well. "We felt that God was near,
and omnipotent to do what seemed best in his sight."[68]

Did ever mother run more quickly to protect her crying child
in danger's hour, than the Lord Jesus hastens to answer believing prayer and send help to His servants *in His own good time
and way, so far as it shall be for His glory and their good?*[69]

---

[65]Ibid., p. 164.

[66]This meant that, in one sense, life was not simple. If God may rescue us for his glory or
let us be killed for his glory, which way to turn in self-preservation is not an easy question to
answer.

    To know what was best to be done, in such trying circumstances, was an abiding
perplexity. To have left altogether, when so surrounded by perils and enemies, at first
seemed the wisest course, and was the repeated advice of many friends. But again, I had
acquired the language, and had gained a considerable influence amongst the Natives,
and there were a number warmly attached both to myself and to the Worship. To have
left would have been to lose all, which to me was heart-rending; therefore, risking all
with Jesus, I held on while the hope of being spared longer had not absolutely and
entirely vanished. (Ibid., p. 173)

[67]Ibid., p. 148. "Often have I seized the pointed barrel and directed it upwards, or, pleading
with my assailant, uncapped his musket in the struggle. At other times, nothing could be said,
nothing done, but stand still in silent prayer, asking to protect us or to prepare us for going
home to His glory. He fulfilled His own promise—'I will not fail thee nor forsake thee'" (ibid.,
pp. 329–330).

[68]Ibid., p. 197.

[69]Ibid., p. 164, emphasis added. Paton taught his helpers to pray this way as well, and we hear
the same faith and prayer in Abraham, his trustworthy Aneityumese servant:

His Courage Came from a Certain Kind of Joy

The joy that made all the difference was the joy in God that he knew could not be surpassed anywhere in any other ministry.

> Oh that the pleasure-seeking men and women of the world could only taste and feel the real joy of those who know and love the true God—a heritage which the world . . . cannot give to them, but which the poorest and humblest followers of Jesus inherit and enjoy![70]

> My heart often says within itself—when, *when* will men's eyes at home be opened? When will the rich and the learned . . . renounce their shallow frivolities, and go to live amongst the poor, the ignorant, the outcast, and the lost, and write their eternal fame on the souls by them blessed and brought to the Savior? Those who have tasted this highest joy, "The joy of the Lord," will never again ask—*Is Life worth living?*[71]

Near the end of his life, he wrote about the joy that carried him forward, and about his hope that his own children would undertake the same mission and find the same joy:

> Let me record my immovable conviction that this is the noblest service in which any human being can spend or be

---

O Lord, our Heavenly Father, they have murdered Thy servants on Erromanga. They have banished the Aneityumese from dark Tanna. And now they want to kill Missi Paton and me.

Our great King, protect us, and make their hearts soft and sweet to Thy Worship. Or, if they are permitted to kill us, do not Thou hate us, but wash us in the blood of Thy dear Son Jesus Christ. . . . Make us two and all Thy servants strong for Thee and for Thy Worship; and if they kill us now, let us die together in Thy good work, like Thy servants Missi Gordon the man and Missi Gordon the woman. (Ibid., p. 171)

[70] Ibid., p. 78.

[71] He goes on to expand the ground of this joy:

Life, any life, would be well spent, under any conceivable conditions, in bringing one human soul to know and love and serve God and His Son, and thereby securing for yourself at least one temple where your name and memory would be held for ever and for ever in affectionate praise—a regenerated Heart in heaven. That fame will prove immortal, when all the poems and monuments and pyramids of Earth have gone into dust. (Ibid., pp. 411–412)

spent; and that, if God gave me back my life to be lived over again, I would without one quiver of hesitation lay it on the altar to Christ, that He might use it as before in similar ministries of love, especially amongst those who have never yet heard the Name of Jesus. Nothing that has been endured, and nothing that can now befall me, makes me tremble—on the contrary, I *deeply rejoice*—when I breathe the prayer that it may please the blessed Lord to turn the hearts of all my children to the Mission Field and that He may open up their way and make it *their pride and joy* to live and die in carrying Jesus and His Gospel into the heart of the Heathen World![72]

Where did the joy of John G. Paton most deeply repose? The answer, it seems, is that it rested most deeply in the experience of personal communion with Jesus Christ mediated through the promise "Behold, I am with you always" (Matthew 28:20). Therefore, the final source of his courage I would mention is this precious fellowship, especially in danger.

HIS COURAGE CAME FROM PERSONAL FELLOWSHIP WITH JESUS

The sweetness of this fellowship reached its highest and deepest point when it was given through the promise of Christ's word to an endangered missionary hovering on the brink of eternity.

The promise had been given precisely in the context of the Great Commission: "Go therefore and make disciples of all nations. . . . And behold, I am with you always, to the end of the age" (Matthew 28:19–20). More than any other promise, this one brought Jesus close and real to John Paton in all his dangers. After the measles epidemic that killed thousands on the islands, and for which the mis-

---
[72]Ibid., p. 444, emphasis added.

sionaries were blamed, he wrote, "During the crisis, I felt generally calm, and firm of soul, standing erect and with my whole weight on the promise 'Lo! I am with you always.' Precious promise! How often I adore Jesus for it, and rejoice in it! Blessed be his name."[73]

The power this promise had to make Christ real to Paton in hours of crisis was unlike any other Scripture or prayer:

> Without that abiding consciousness of the presence and power of my dear Lord and Savior, nothing else in all the world could have preserved me from losing my reason and perishing miserably. In His words, "Lo, I am with you always, even unto the end of the world," became to me so real that it would not have startled me to behold Him, as Stephen did, gazing down upon the scene. I felt His support-ing power. . . . It is the sober truth, and it comes back to me sweetly after 20 years, that I had my nearest and dearest glimpses of the face and smiles of my blessed Lord in those dread moments when musket, club, or spear was being lev-eled at my life.[74] Oh the bliss of living and enduring, as see-ing "Him who is invisible"![75]

One of the most powerful paragraphs in his *Autobiography* describes his experience of hiding in a tree, at the mercy of an unreliable chief, as hundreds of angry natives hunted him for his life. What he experienced there was the deepest source of Paton's joy and courage. In fact, I would dare to say that to share this experience and call others to enjoy it was the reason that he wrote the story of his life.[76]

---

[73]Ibid., p. 154.

[74]"My constant custom was, in order to prevent war, to run right in between the contending parties. My faith enabled me to grasp and realize the promise, 'Lo, I am with you alway.' In Jesus I felt invulnerable and immortal, so long as I was doing his work. And I can truly say, that these were the moments when I felt my Savior to be most truly and sensibly present, inspiring and empowering me." Ibid., p. 342.

[75]Ibid., p. 117.

[76]"I pity from the depth of my heart every human being, who, from whatever cause, is a stranger to the most ennobling, uplifting, and consoling experience that can come to the soul

He began his *Autobiography* with the words, "What I write here is for the glory of God."[77] That is true. But God gets glory when his *Son* is exalted. And his Son is exalted when we cherish him above all things, especially when "all things" are about to be snatched from us, including our life on earth. That is what this story is about. Here is the story of Paton in the tree.

> Being entirely at the mercy of such doubtful and vacillating friends, I, though perplexed, felt it best to obey. I climbed into the tree and was left there alone in the bush. The hours I spent there live all before me as if it were but of yesterday. I heard the frequent discharging of muskets, and the yells of the Savages. Yet I sat there among the branches, as safe as in the arms of Jesus. Never, in all my sorrows, did my Lord draw nearer to me, and speak more soothingly in my soul, than when the moonlight flickered among those chestnut leaves, and the night air played on my throbbing brow, as I told all my heart to Jesus. Alone, yet not alone! If it be to glorify my God, I will not grudge to spend many nights alone in such a tree, to feel again my Savior's spiritual presence, to enjoy His consoling fellowship. If thus thrown back upon your own soul, alone, all alone, in the midnight, in the bush, in the very embrace of death itself, have you a Friend that will not fail you then?[78]

"Have You a Friend That Will Not Fail You?"

This is the question that Paton leaves in our ears. Jesus came into the world to befriend sinners. His enemies accused him of this and spoke more truly than they knew. They called him "a glutton and a drunkard, a friend of tax collectors and sinners!" (Matthew

---

of man—blessed communion with the Father of our Spirits, through gracious union with the Lord Jesus Christ." Ibid., p. 359.
[77]Ibid., p. 2.
[78]Ibid., p. 200.

11:19). But Jesus knew who needed the physician—the sick. And if they would have him heal the deep disease of their sin, he would have them as his friend. "No longer do I call you servants, for the servant does not know what his master is doing; but I have called you friends" (John 15:15).

The features of friendship that Jesus focused on in this relationship were, first, that he laid down his life to save his friends. "Greater love has no one than this, that someone lay down his life for his friends" (John 15:13); and, second, friends of the Master know what he is doing (v. 15). They are part of the inner ring of the Great Planner. This means that the friendship of Jesus is woven into his mission. His friends understand what he is up to in the world.

And they not only understand, they agree. They are on board with the plan. Friends don't just sit and look at each other. They link arms and pursue a common cause. "You are my friends if you do what I command you" (v. 14). If Jesus is the Supreme Lord as well as the Best Friend, it cannot be otherwise. Servants do what the master says because they have to. Friends do it because they want to. And they want to because they have been taken into the council chamber. They have been shown the greatness of the plan and the greatness of the victory. They are thrilled to be with Jesus in this great global mission.

It will be a costly mission. There will be afflictions all along the way. That is the appointed path to triumph. So Paton leaves us with his question: "If thus thrown back upon your own soul, alone, all alone, in the midnight, in the bush, in the very embrace of death itself, have you a Friend that will not fail you then?"

3

ADONIRAM JUDSON

"How Few There Are Who Die So Hard":
The Cost of Bringing Christ to Burma

The story of Adoniram Judson's losses is almost overwhelming. Just when you think the last one was the worst, and he could endure no more, another comes. In fact, it would be overwhelming if we could not see it all from God's long historical view. The seed that died a thousand times has given life in Myanmar (Burma) to an extraordinary movement to Christ.

The Fruit of His Affliction

When Adoniram Judson entered Burma in July 1813, it was a hostile and utterly unreached place. William Carey had told Judson in India a few months earlier not to go there. Today it probably would have been considered a closed country—with anarchic despotism, fierce war with Siam, enemy raids, constant rebellion, and no religious toleration. All the previous missionaries had died or left.[1]

But Judson went there with his twenty-three-year-old wife of seventeen months. He was twenty-four years old, and he worked there for thirty-eight years until his death at age sixty-one, with

[1] Courtney Anderson, *To the Golden Shore: The Life of Adoniram Judson* (Grand Rapids, MI: Zondervan, 1956), p. 134.

one trip home to New England after thirty-three years. The price he paid was immense. He was a seed that fell into the ground and died again and again. And the fruit God gave is celebrated even in scholarly works like David Barrett's *World Christian Encyclopedia*: "The largest Christian force in Burma is the Burma Baptist Convention, which owes its origin to the pioneering activity of the American Baptist missionary Adoniram Judson."[2] At the turn from the second to the third millennium, Patrick Johnstone estimated the Myanmar (Burma's new name) Baptist Convention to be 3,700 congregations with 617,781 members and 1,900,000 affiliates[3]—the fruit of this dead seed.

Of course, there were others besides Adoniram Judson— hundreds of others over time. They too came and gave away their lives. Many of them died much younger than Judson. They only serve to make the point. The astonishing fruit in Myanmar today has grown in the soil of the suffering and death of many missionaries, especially Adoniram Judson.

One question that moves my study and prayer and writing of this book is: If Christ delays his return another 200 years—a mere fraction of a day in his reckoning—which of us who are alive today will have suffered and died so that the triumphs of grace will be told about one of the 3,500 people groups who are in the same condition today that the Karen, Chin, Kachin, and Burmese were in 1813? Who will labor so long and so hard and so perseveringly that in 200 years there will be two million Christians in many of the 10/40-window peoples who at that time will scarcely be able to recall their Muslim or Hindu or Buddhist roots?

---

[2]David Barrett, ed., *World Christian Encyclopedia* (New York: Oxford University Press, 1982), p. 202.
[3]Patrick Johnstone and Jason Mandryk, eds., *Operation World* (Carlisle, UK: Paternoster, 2001), p. 462.

May God use the life of Adoniram Judson to stir many of us to give our lives to this great cause!

Deep Faith in the Sovereignty of God

Adoniram Judson lived on the great truths of God's sovereign grace. He would have been known as a Calvinist, but not the kind that wears his Calvinism on his sleeve.[4] You can see the evidence for his Reformed convictions in Thomas J. Nettles's *By His Grace and for His Glory*.[5]

His father, who was a pastor of the Third Congregational Church of Plymouth, Massachusetts, had studied with Jonathan Edwards's student Joseph Bellamy. Five years after his son had left for Asia, the father became convinced of the Baptist way and risked his livelihood by resigning from his Congregational church. Adoniram, as we will see, received from his father both the Reformed theology and the courage to put his life on the line rather than compromise his beliefs.

The importance this has for our purpose here is to stress that this deep confidence in God's overarching providence through all calamity and misery sustained him to the end. He said, "If I had not felt certain that every additional trial was ordered by infinite love and mercy, I could not have survived my accumulated sufferings."[6] He loved what he called "the Doctrines of Grace." What he saw in them was the power for sacrifice and self-denial, not the ammunition for argument. "That faith which consists

---

[4]Erroll Hulse, *Adoniram Judson and the Missionary Call* (Leeds, UK: Reformation Today Trust, 1996), p. 48. "When we come to the doctrines of grace we find that he believed them implicitly rather than by explicit exposition."

[5]Thomas J. Nettles, *By His Grace and for His Glory* (Grand Rapids, MI: Baker, 1986), pp. 148–154.

[6]Quoted in Eugene Myers Harrison, *Giants of the Missionary Trail* (Chicago: Scripture Press Foundation, 1954), p. 73.

merely in a correct belief of the Doctrines of Grace and prompts no self denial . . . is no faith at all."[7]

This was the unshakable confidence of all three of his wives, Ann (also called Nancy), Sarah, and Emily. For example, Ann, who married Judson on February 5, 1812, and left with him on the boat for Asia on February 19 at age twenty-three, bore three children to Adoniram. All of them died. The first baby, nameless, was born dead just as they sailed from India to Burma. The second child, Roger Williams Judson, lived seventeen months and died. The third, Maria Elizabeth Butterworth Judson, lived to be two and outlived her mother by six months and then died.

When her second child died, Ann Judson wrote:

> Our hearts were bound up with this child; we felt he was our earthly all, our only source of innocent recreation in this heathen land. But God saw it was necessary to remind us of our error, and to strip us of our only little all. O, may it not be vain that he has done it. May we so improve it that he will stay his hand and say "It is enough."[8]

In other words, what sustained this man and his three wives was a rock-solid confidence that God is sovereign and God is good. And all things come from his hand for the good—sometimes the incredibly *painful* good—of his children.

The Roots of Confidence in God's Good Providence

There are roots of this missionary-sustaining confidence in God's goodness and providence. One, as we have seen, is the legacy that his father left him. That's what his father believed, and that's what

---

[7]Nettles, *By His Grace and for His Glory*, p. 154.
[8]Anderson, *To the Golden Shore*, p. 193.

he lived. A second source of this confidence was the Bible. Judson was a lover of the word of God. The main legacy of his thirty-eight years in Burma was a complete translation of the Bible into Burmese and a dictionary that all the later missionaries could use.

Once when a Buddhist teacher said that he could not believe that Christ suffered the death of the cross because no king allows his son such indignity, Judson responded,

> Therefore you are not a disciple of Christ. A true disciple inquires not whether a fact is agreeable to his own reason, but whether it is in the book. His pride has yielded to the divine testimony. Teacher, your pride is still unbroken. Break down your pride, and yield to the word of God.[9]

The Bible was a friend closer and more lasting than his wife. When the bottom fell out some years later and he struggled with the darkest spiritual depression, he disappeared into the tiger-infested jungle to live alone. But he did not leave his Bible behind. This unbreakable attachment to the Bible saved his life and defined the final outcome.

A Remarkable Conversion

A third source of his confidence in the goodness and detailed providence of God was the way God saved him. It is a remarkable story. He was a brilliant boy. His mother taught him to read in one week when he was three to surprise his father when he came home from a trip.[10] He read his father a chapter from the Bible to surprise him.

---

[9]Ibid., p. 240.
[10]Ibid., p. 14.

When he was sixteen he entered Brown University as a sopho-more and graduated at the top of his class three years later in 1807. What his godly parents didn't know was that Adoniram was being lured away from the faith by a fellow student named Jacob Eames, who was a deist. By the time Judson was finished, he had no Christian faith. He kept this concealed from his parents until his twentieth birthday, August 9, 1808, when he broke their hearts with his announcement that he had no faith and that he intended to go to New York and learn to write for the theater—which he did six days later, riding on a horse his father gave him as part of his inheritance.

It didn't prove to be the life of his dreams. He attached him-self to some strolling players and, as he said later, lived "a reck-less, vagabond life, finding lodgings where he could, and bilking the landlord where he found opportunity."[11] His disgust with what he found there was the beginning of several remarkable providences.

He went to visit his Uncle Ephraim in Sheffield but found there instead "a pious young man" who stunned him by being firm in his Christian convictions without being "austere and dictatorial."[12] Strange that he should find this young man there instead of his uncle.

The next night he stayed in a small village inn where he had never been before. The innkeeper apologized that his sleep might be interrupted because there was a man critically ill in the next room. Through the night he heard comings and goings and low voices and groans and gasps. It bothered him to think that the man next to him may not be prepared to die. He wondered about

---

[11]Ibid., p. 193.
[12]Ibid., p. 42.

himself and had terrible thoughts of his own dying. He felt foolish because good deists weren't supposed to have these struggles.

When he was leaving in the morning, he asked if the man next door was better. "He is dead," said the innkeeper. Judson was struck with the finality of it all. On his way out he asked, "Do you know who he was?" "Oh yes. Young man from the college in Providence. Name was Eames, Jacob Eames."[13]

Judson could hardly move. He stayed there for hours pondering the death of his unbelieving friend. If Eames were right, then this was a meaningless event. But Judson could not believe it. "That hell should open in that country inn and snatch Jacob Eames, his dearest friend and guide, from the next bed—this could not, simply could not, be pure coincidence."[14] His conversion was not immediate. But now it was sure that God was on his trail—like the apostle Paul on the Damascus Road—and there was no escape. Months of struggle were to follow.

The Path to Marriage

He entered Andover Seminary in October 1808 and on December 2 made solemn dedication of himself to God. The fire was burning for missions at Andover and at Williams College. (The Haystack Prayer Meeting had taken place in August 1806 near Williams College, and two from there had come to Andover.)

On June 28, 1810, Judson and others presented themselves to the Congregationalists for missionary service in the East. He met Ann Hasseltine that same day and fell in love. After knowing

[13]Ibid., p. 44. The source of this story is oral reports from family members recorded in Francis Wayland, *A Memoir of the Life and Labors of the Rev. Adoniram Judson, D.D.*, 2 vols. (Boston: Phillips, Sampson, and Co., 1854), 1:24–25.
[14]Anderson, *To the Golden Shore*, p. 45.

Ann for one month, he declared his intention to become a suitor and wrote to her father the following letter:

> I have now to ask, whether you can consent to part with your daughter early next spring, to see her no more in this world; whether you can consent to her departure, and her subjection to the hardships and sufferings of missionary life; whether you can consent to her exposure to the dangers of the ocean, to the fatal influence of the southern climate of India; to every kind of want and distress; to degradation, insult, persecution, and perhaps a violent death. Can you consent to all this, for the sake of him who left his heavenly home, and died for her and for you; for the sake of perishing, immortal souls; for the sake of Zion, and the glory of God? Can you consent to all this, in hope of soon meeting your daughter in the world of glory, with the crown of righteousness, brightened with the acclamations of praise which shall redound to her Savior from heathens saved, through her means, from eternal woe and despair?[15]

Her father, amazingly, said she could make up her own mind. She wrote to her friend Lydia Kimball:

> I feel willing, and expect, if nothing in Providence prevents, to spend my days in this world in heathen lands. Yes, Lydia, I have about come to the determination to give up all my comforts and enjoyments here, sacrifice my affection to relatives and friends, and go where God, in his Providence, shall see fit to place me.[16]

Between this engagement and the marriage, Judson made a trip to London to seek support from the London Missionary Society.

---

[15]Ibid., p. 83.
[16]Ibid., p. 84.

Instead of support of that sort, he discovered the kind of support he would need far more. The ship he was on, the British *Packet*, was taken by a French ship, *L'Invincible Napoleon*, and Judson was made prisoner with the crew. He was taken to Bayonne, France, and put in prison.

In this helpless situation for a twenty-two-year-old American, Judson learned of a kind of provision he would need again and again in Burma. Amazingly, a man from Philadelphia snuck Judson out of the prison by bribing the guards. He made his way to London and made his futile effort to solicit the support of the London Missionary Society. He left on June 18, 1811, and arrived in New York August 7 from a journey that seemed pointless—except for this: He always "regarded his detention in France as a very important, and, indeed, necessary part of his preparation for the duties which afterwards devolved upon him."[17]

Adoniram and Ann were married six months later on February 5, 1812, and sailed for India fourteen days later with two other couples and two single men[18] divided among two ships, in case one went down.

The Path to India and the Baptist Way

The voyage to India took 114 days. On the journey, Judson had been studying the issue of baptism and was becoming convinced from Scripture that his views on infant baptism were not biblical. In India, he and Ann lived for a short time with William Carey. In this context, Judson settled his views and became a Baptist. Ann followed, as did one of the single missionary men, Luther Rice.

---

[17]Ibid., p. 93
[18]Luther Rice, Gordon Hall, Samuel and Harriet Newell, Samuel and Roxana Nott.

This was a heart-wrenching and life-threatening decision at several levels. Ann expressed the internal doctrinal and emotional struggle for both of them:

> I . . . must acknowledge that the face of Scripture does favor the Baptist sentiments. I intend to persevere in examining the subject. And [I] hope that I shall be disposed to embrace the truth, whatever it may be. It is painfully mortifying to my natural feelings, to think seriously of renouncing a system which I have been taught from infancy to believe and respect, and embrace one which I have been taught to despise. O that the Spirit of God may enlighten and direct my mind—may prevent my retaining an old error, or embracing a new one![19]

Moreover, they had been sent out by a Congregational board. Their support would very likely not be continued. And perhaps worst of all was that this change split the group of missionaries who went out together. They loved each other, and as Ann said, "We are perfectly united with our brethren in every other respect, and are much attached to them."[20] But how would they plant and structure a church when their views on baptism differed so much? Ann captured the situation and the cost with these words:

> Thus, we are confirmed Baptists, not because we wanted to be, but because truth compelled us to be. We have endeavored to count the cost, and be prepared for the many severe trials resulting from this change of sentiment. We anticipate the loss of reputation, and of the affection and esteem of many of our American friends. But the most trying circum-

---

[19]Anderson, *To the Golden Shore*, pp. 144–145.
[20]Ibid., p. 144.

stances attending this change, and that which has caused us most pain, is the separation which must take place between us and our dear missionary associates. . . . We feel that we are alone in the world, with no real friend but each other, no one on whom we can depend but God.[21]

As with all events under God's merciful providence, this painful circumstance had some remarkably positive effects. The Judsons and Rice knew that someone would need to go home to make official the departure from the Congregational oversight and seek support from the Baptists. Rice was single, and it made sense for him to return. He entered New York harbor in September 1813. From that time until he died in 1836, he became a stateside advocate for Baptist Missions. He never returned to join the Judsons. His labor gave cohesion to the Baptist movement in America and gave support to Baptist missions abroad.[22] His influence was extraordinary.

The story would be very different for Adoniram and Ann Judson. After a time in India, they chose to take the risks of venturing to a new field. They arrived in Rangoon, Burma, on July 13, 1813.

The Beginnings of Their Sufferings

There began a lifelong battle in 108-degree heat with cholera, malaria, dysentery, and unknown miseries that would take two of Judson's wives, seven of his thirteen children, and colleague after colleague in death.

---

[21]Ibid., p. 146.
[22]Largely owing to the untiring advocacy by Luther Rice for Baptist unity and missions, Baptists met for their first national gathering at Philadelphia in May 1814. It was called "The General Missionary Convention of the Baptist Denomination in United States of America, for Foreign Missions."

The first news from home arrived two years later on September 5, 1815. They had died to the nearness of family. Adoniram would never see his mother or father or brother again. He would not return for thirty-three years. "Missionary time" in those days was very slow. It was a world of difference from today. If someone was sick enough, the typical remedy to save the life was a sea voyage. So a marriage or the entire work could be put on hold, so to speak, for three to six months as someone was sent out to sea.

Or it could be longer. Eight years into their mission, Ann was so ill that the only hope was a trip home. She sailed on August 21, 1821. She returned on December 5, 1823, two years and four months later. And when she arrived, Judson had not heard from her for ten months. If you are married and you love your wife, and you are both called to the Great Work, this is the way you die day after day for a greater good and a greater joy.

One of the joys was seeing some of God's goodness in the dark providences. For example, when Ann was recovering in the States, she wrote a book titled *An Account of the American Baptist Mission to the Burman Empire*. It had a huge influence in stirring up recruits and prayer and finances. This would have never happened without her sickness and two-year absence. But most of the time, God's wise purposes in their pain were not that clear.

The Price of Breakthrough

Through all the struggles with sickness and interruptions, Judson labored to learn the language, translate the Bible, and do evangelism on the streets. Six years after they arrived, they baptized their first convert, Maung Nau. The sowing was long and hard, the reaping even harder for years. But in 1831, nineteen years after their arrival, there was a new spirit in the land. Judson wrote:

> The spirit of inquiry . . . is spreading everywhere, through the whole length and breadth of the land." [We have distributed] nearly 10,000 tracts, giving to none but those who ask. I presume there have been 6000 applications at the house. Some come two or three months' journey, from the borders of Siam and China—"Sir, we hear that there is an eternal hell. We are afraid of it. Do give us a writing that will tell us how to escape it." Others, from the frontiers of Kathay, 100 miles north of Ava—"Sir, we have seen a writing that tells about an eternal God. Are you the man that gives away such writings? If so, pray give us one, for we want to know the truth before we die." Others, from the interior of the country, where the name of Jesus Christ is a little known—"Are you Jesus Christ's man? Give us a writing that tells us about Jesus Christ."[23]

But there had been an enormous price to pay between the first convert in 1819 and this outpouring of God's power in 1831.

In 1823, Adoniram and Ann moved from Rangoon to Ava, the capital, about three hundred miles inland and further up the Irrawaddy River. It was risky to be that near the despotic emperor. In May of the next year, a British fleet arrived in Rangoon and bombarded the harbor. All Westerners were immediately viewed as spies, and Adoniram was dragged from his home. On June 8, 1824, he was put in prison. His feet were fettered, and at night a long horizontal bamboo pole was lowered and passed between the fettered legs and hoisted up until only the shoulder and heads of the prisoners rested on the ground.

---

[23]Anderson, *To the Golden Shore*, pp. 398–399.

Years later when his wife was dealing with deep darkness in her own soul, he recounted to her that he kept his sanity during the prison months partly by reciting repeatedly the lines of William Cowper,

> Beware of desp'rate steps; the darkest day
> (Live till tomorrow) will have passed away.[24]

As horrible as the conditions were in prison, Judson was spared his reason. He could still think through the possibilities of how this would all work out for the advancement of the gospel. He said to a fellow prisoner named Gouger,

> Here I have been ten years preaching the gospel to timid listeners who wish to embrace the truth but dare not, and beseeching the Emperor to grant liberty of conscience to his people but without success, and now when all human means seem at an end, God opens the way by leading a Christian nation to subdue the country. It is possible my life will be spared; if so, with what ardor shall I pursue my work! If not—his will be done. The door will be opened for others who would do the work better.[25]

Ann was pregnant, but she walked the two miles daily to the palace to plead that Judson was not a spy and that they should have mercy. She got some relief for him so that he could come out into a courtyard. The prisoners got vermin in their hair amid the rotting food and had to be shaved bald. Almost a year later, they were suddenly moved to a more distant village prison, gaunt, with hollow eyes, dressed in rags, crippled from the torture. There

---

[24] William Cowper, "The Needless Alarm, Moral" (1794).
[25] Anderson, To the Golden Shore, pp. 333–334.

the mosquitoes from the rice paddies almost drove them mad on their bloody feet.

The daughter, Maria, had been born by now, and Ann was almost as sick and thin as Adoniram, but she still pursued him, with her baby, to take care of him as she could. Her milk dried up, and the jailer had mercy on them and actually let Judson take the baby each evening into the village fettered and beg for women to nurse his baby.

On November 4, 1825, Judson was suddenly released. The government needed him as a translator in negotiations with Britain. The long ordeal was over—seventeen months in prison and on the brink of death, with his wife sacrificing herself and her baby to care for him as she could. Ann's health was broken. Eleven months later she died (October 24, 1826). And six months later their daughter died (April 24, 1827).

When the Darkness Does Not Lift

While he was suffering in prison, Adoniram had been sustained with hope and with a spirit deeply submissive to the providence of God. We heard it in the words to his fellow prisoner: "It is possible my life will be spared; if so, with what ardor shall I pursue my work! If not—his will be done. The door will be opened for others who would do the work better."[26] But now that his wife and daughter were gone, darkness began to settle over his soul. Then in July, three months after the death of his little girl, he got word that his father had died eight months earlier.

The psychological effect of these losses was devastating. Self-doubt overtook his mind, and he wondered if he had become a

---

[26]Ibid., p. 334.

missionary for ambition and fame, not humility and self-denying love. He began to read Catholic mystics like Madame Guyon, Fenelon, and Thomas à Kempis who led him into solitary asceticism and various forms of self-mortification. He dropped his Old Testament translation work, the love of his life, and retreated more and more from people and from "anything that might conceivably support pride or promote his pleasure."[27]

He refused to eat outside the mission. He destroyed all letters of commendation. He formally renounced the honorary Doctor of Divinity that Brown University had given him in 1823 by writing a letter to the *American Baptist Magazine*. He gave all his private wealth (about six thousand dollars) to the Baptist Board. He asked that his salary be reduced by one quarter and promised to give more to missions himself. In October 1828, he built a hut in the jungle some distance from the Moulmein mission house and moved in on October 24, 1828, the second anniversary of Ann's death, to live in total isolation.

He wrote in one letter home to Ann's relatives, "My tears flow at the same time over the forsaken grave of my dear love and over the loathsome sepulcher of my own heart."[28] He had a grave dug beside the hut and sat beside it contemplating the stages of the body's dissolution. He ordered all his letters in New England destroyed. He refused to return a legal document his sister needed unless his demand were carried out. He retreated for forty days alone further into the tiger-infested jungle and wrote in one letter that he felt utter spiritual desolation. "God is to me the Great Unknown. I believe in him, but I find him not."[29]

His brother Elnathan died May 8, 1829, at the age of thirty-

----

[27]Ibid., p. 387.
[28]Ibid., p. 388.
[29]Ibid., p. 391.

five. Paradoxically, this proved the turning point of Judson's recovery, because he had reason to believe that the brother that he had left in unbelief seventeen years earlier had died in faith. All through the year of 1830, Adoniram was climbing out of his darkness.

Recall that it was 1831—the next year—when he experienced the great outpouring of spiritual interest across the land. "The spirit of inquiry . . . is spreading everywhere, through the whole length and breadth of the land."[30] Is that a coincidence? Or is that a God-ordained pattern for spiritual breakthrough in a dark and unreached place?

A Finished Bible and a New Wife

Central to his missionary labors from the beginning, and especially at this juncture in his life, was the translation of the Bible. Judson knew the original languages and worked from the Greek and Hebrew. Four years after he arrived in Burma (May 1817), he had completed the Gospel of Matthew, and then began work on a Burmese dictionary.

Now in these years without a wife and children, he confined himself to a small room built for the purpose of being able to devote almost all his energy to refining the New Testament translation and pressing on with the Old Testament. At the end of 1832, three thousand copies of the completed New Testament were printed. He finished the Old Testament on January 31, 1834, and wrote on that day:

> Thanks be to God, I can now say I have attained. I have knelt down before him, with the last leaf in my hand, and

---

[30]Ibid., p. 398.

imploring his forgiveness for all the sins which have pol-
luted my efforts in this department, and his aid in future
efforts to remove the errors and imperfections which neces-
sarily cleave to the work, I have commended it to his mercy
and grace; I have dedicated it to his glory. May he make his
own inspired word, now complete in the Burman tongue,
the grand instrument of filling all Burma with songs of
praise to our great God and Savior Jesus Christ. Amen.[31]

With the first draft of the Bible in Burmese complete, it seems
as though God smiled on these labors with the favor of a new
wife. Three years earlier, another missionary in Burma named
George Boardman had died. His widow Sarah stayed in Burma
and became a legend in her own right, pressing into the interior
with her baby George.[32] In February 1834, Judson received a letter from Sarah. On April 1, he left Moulmein for Tavoy resolved
to court her. On April 10, they were married. Judson wrote in
his journal about their two departed spouses and their new love:

> Once more, farewell to thee, Boardman, and thy long-
> cherished grave. May thy memory be ever fresh and fra-
> grant, as the memory of the other beloved, whose beautiful,
> death-marred form reposes at the foot of the hopia tree.
> May we, the survivors, so live as to deserve and receive the
> smiles of the sainted ones who have gone before us. And at
> last may we all four be reunited before the throne of glory,
> and form a peculiarly happy family, our mutual loves all
> purified and consummated in the bright world of love.[33]

These were to be some of his happiest times in Burma, but not
without pain, and not to last much more than a decade. "She

---

[31]Ibid., p. 411.
[32]Ibid., p. 402.
[33]Ibid., p. 414.

was a blue eyed beauty and he at 47 had a full head of hair with no gray and was strong and healthy and was coming it seemed into a season of peace and joy with Sarah."[34] She would bear Adoniram eight children. Five of them would live beyond their childhood.

After marriage to Sarah, Adoniram gave himself to the revision of the Old Testament and, for a season, preached seven messages a week, one on Sunday morning and one on the other evenings of the week.[35] Sarah was a gifted partner and knew the language better than any but Judson himself. She translated *Pilgrim's Progress* during these years before her untimely death.

Another Wife Given Up in Death

After bearing eight children in eleven years, Sarah became so ill that the family decided to travel to America in the hopes that the sea air would work healing. They set sail April 26, 1845, with their three oldest children and the intention of leaving them for education in the United States when they returned. They left the three youngest behind, one of whom died before Judson returned.

Judson had not been to America now for thirty-three years and was only returning for the sake of his wife. As they rounded the tip of Africa in September 1845, Sarah died. Adoniram recorded her dying on the ship in tender detail:

> Her mind became liable to wander; but a single word was sufficient to recall and steady her recollection. On the evening of the 31st of August, she appeared to be drawing near

[34]Ibid., p. 417.
[35]Ibid., p. 418.

to the end of her pilgrimage. The children took leave of her, and retired to rest. I sat alone to the side of her bed during the hours of the night, endeavoring to administer relief to the distressed body, and consolation to the departing soul. At 2 o'clock in the morning, wishing to obtain one more token of recognition, I roused her attention, and said "Do you still love the Savior?" "O, yes," she replied, "I ever love the Lord Jesus Christ." I said again, "Do you still love me?" She replied in the affirmative by a peculiar expression of her own. "Then give me one more kiss," and we exchanged that token of love for the last time. Another hour passed, life continued to recede, and she ceased to breathe. For a moment I traced her upward flight, and thought of the wonders which were opening to her view. I then closed her sightless eyes, dressed her, for the last time, in the drapery of death; and being quite exhausted with many sleepless nights, I threw myself down and slept.[36]

The ship dropped anchor at St. Helena Island long enough to dig a grave and bury a wife and mother and then sail on. This time Adoniram did not descend into the depths of depression as before. He had his children. But even more, his sufferings had disengaged him from hoping for too much in this world. He was learning how to "hate his life" in this world (John 12:25) without bitterness or depression.

He had one passion: to return and give his life for Burma. So he planned for his stay in the States to be just long enough to get his children settled and find a ship back. All that was left of the life he knew in New England was his sister. She had kept his room exactly as it had been thirty-three years earlier and would keep it that way to the day she died.

---

[36]Ibid., p. 440.

He landed Wednesday, October 15, 1845. His first wife's book *An Account of the American Baptist Mission to the Burman Empire* and the publishing of the *Memoir of Mrs. Ann Judson* by James Knowles in 1829 had been read by hundreds of thousands. Adoniram Judson was a celebrity. Countless parents had named their children after him. He had been the topic of thousands of sermons. His homecoming was a sensation.

God Planned Another Marriage, But Not a Long One

Judson's stay in the States did not go according to plan. To everyone's amazement, he fell in love a third time, this time with Emily Chubbuck, and married her on June 2, 1846. She was twenty-nine; he was fifty-seven. She was a famous writer and left her fame and writing career to go with Judson to Burma.[37] They arrived in November 1846. And God gave them four of the happiest years that either of them had ever known. On their first anniversary (June 2, 1847), she wrote,

> It has been far the happiest year of my life; and, what is in my eyes still more important, my husband says it has been among the happiest of his. . . . I never met with any man who could talk so well, day after day, on every subject, religious, literary, scientific, political, and—nice baby-talk.[38]

They had one child. Things looked bright, but then the old sicknesses attacked Adoniram one last time. The only hope was to send the desperately ill Judson on a voyage. On April 3, 1850,

---

[37]Emily's pen name was Fanny Forester. She had "skyrocketed to literary fame" with a children's book called *Charles Linn* and another book, *Trippings in Author Land*. When Judson met her he said, "How can you reconcile it with your conscience to employ such noble talents in writing so little useful and spiritual as those sketches I read?" He resolved that she should write Sarah's memoir and that she should be his next wife. Ibid., p. 454.
[38]Ibid., p. 391.

they carried Adoniram onto *The Aristide Marie* bound for the Isle of France with one friend, Thomas Ranney, to care for him. In his misery, he would be roused from time to time by terrible pain ending in vomiting. One of his last sentences was, "How few there are who . . . who die so hard!"[39]

At 4:15 on Friday afternoon, April 12, 1850, Adoniram Judson died at sea, away from all his family and the Burmese church. That evening the ship hove to.

> The crew assembled quietly. The larboard port was opened. There were no prayers. . . . The captain gave the order. The coffin slid through the port into the night. The location was latitude 13 degrees North, longitude 93 degrees East, almost in the eastward shadow of the Andaman Islands, and only a few hundred miles west of the mountains of Burma. The Aristide Marie sailed on toward the Isle of France.[40]

Ten days later, Emily gave birth to their second child who died at birth. She learned four months later that her husband was dead. She returned to New England that next January and died of tuberculosis three years later at the age of thirty-seven.

The Burmese Bible was done. The dictionary was done. Hundreds of converts were leading the church. And today there are about 3,700 congregations of Baptists in Myanmar who trace their origin to this man's labors of love.

A Plea to Be a Part of What Judson and Christ Died For

Life is fleeting. In a very short time, we will all give an account before Jesus Christ, not only as to how well we have fulfilled our

---

[39]Ibid., p. 504.
[40]Ibid., p. 505.

vocations, but how well we have obeyed the command to make disciples of all nations.

Many of the peoples of the world are without any indigenous Christian movement today. Christ is not enthroned there, his grace is unknown there, and people are perishing with no access to the gospel. Most of these hopeless peoples do not want followers of Jesus to come. At least they think they don't. They are hostile to Christian missions. Today this is the final frontier. And the Lord still says, "Behold, I am sending you out as sheep in the midst of wolves. . . . [S]ome of you they will put to death. You will be hated by all for my name's sake. But not a hair of your head will perish" (Matthew 10:16; Luke 21:16–18).

Are you sure that God wants you to keep doing what you are doing? For most of you, he probably does. Your calling is radical obedience for the glory of Christ right where you are. But for many of you, the stories in this book are among a hundred things God is using to loosen your roots and plant you in another place. Some of you he is calling to fill up what is lacking in the sufferings of Christ, to fall like a grain of wheat into some distant ground and die, to hate your life in this world and so to keep it forever and bear much fruit. Judson wrote to missionary candidates in 1832:

> Bear in mind, that a large proportion of those who come out on a mission to the East die within five years after leaving their native land. Walk softly, therefore; death is narrowly watching your steps.[41]

The question is not whether we will die, but whether we will die in a way that bears much fruit.

---

[41]Adoniram Judson, "Advice to Missionary Candidates," Maulmain, June 25, 1832, http://www.wholesomewords.org/missions/bjudson4.html; accessed 05-21-08.

CONCLUSION

THIS MOMENTARY AFFLICTION
FOR ETERNAL GLORY

The position we are in at the beginning of the twenty-first century is one that cries out for tremendous missionary effort and great missionary sacrifice. Patrick Johnstone writes in *Operation World* that only in the 1990s did we get a reasonably complete listing of the world's peoples. For the first time, we can see clearly what is left to be done.

There are about 12,000 ethnolinguistic[1] peoples in the world. About 3,500 of these peoples have, on average, 1.2 percent Christian populations—about twenty million of the 1.7 billion people in these groups, using the broadest, nominal definition of Christian.[2] Most of these least reached 3,500 peoples are in the 10/40 window[3] and are religiously unsympathetic to Christian missions. That means that we—the body of Christ, from the West and from the Global South[4]—must go to these peoples with

---

[1] The term *ethnolinguistic* is used to designate people groups categorized by ethnicity and language, in distinction from the term *geopolitical* that has reference to peoples categorized according to political and geographic boundaries.

[2] Patrick Johnstone, Jason Mandryk, eds., *Operation World* (Carlisle, UK: Paternoster, 2001), pp. 15–16.

[3] A term representing a huge swathe of territory from the west coast of Africa to the eastern edge of south Asia and from 10 degrees north to 40 degrees north. You can see a map of the region and keep up with the ever-changing picture of unreached peoples at http://www.joshua project.net/10-40-window.php.

[4] *Global South* is a relatively new term that tries to capture the reality that a map of the "statistical center of gravity of global Christianity shows that center moving steadily southward, from a point in northern Italy in 1800, to central Spain in 1900, to Morocco by 1970, and to a point near Timbuktu [in Mali, West Africa] today [2006]. The Southward trajectory will continue unchecked through the coming century" (Philip Jenkins, *The New Faces of Christianity: Believing the Bible in the Global South* [Oxford: Oxford University Press, 2006], p. 9). In other words, without an astonishing spiritual awakening and reformation to reverse the trends of the past century, the centers of vitality and influence and mission sending will increasingly

the gospel. There is no indigenous church capable of evangelizing its own people in these groups. That's what it means to be *unreached*. Where a faithful indigenous church exists, the role of outsiders is humble partnership and helpfulness. But that is not the case for these unreached peoples. Reaching them, as Jesus commands, will be dangerous and costly. Some of us, and some of our children, will be killed.

The Lure to Leave the Hardship

The temptation under these circumstances will be to give up. This has always been the case. Sitting in my comfortable study in Minneapolis, it is too easy for me to plead for perseverance in suffering for the sake of the nations. I pray that I am always willing to be endangered for Christ and his kingdom. I know that mine, for now, is a relatively secure ministry. But others have given the plea for perseverance more authentically than I. Here is the way Adoniram Judson put it in a letter that he wrote to missionaries on June 25, 1832:

> Beware of the greater reaction which will take place after you have acquired the language, and become fatigued and worn out with preaching the gospel to a disobedient and gainsaying people. You will sometimes long for a quiet retreat, where you can find a respite from the tug of toiling at native work—the incessant, intolerable friction of the missionary grindstone. And Satan will sympathize with you in this matter; and he will present some chapel of ease, in which to officiate in your native tongue, some government situation, some professorship or editorship, some literary

---

move from the traditional points of power in Europe and America to South America, Africa, and Asia.

or scientific pursuit, some supernumerary translation, or, at least, some system of schools; anything, in a word, that will help you, without much surrender of character, to slip out of real missionary work. Such a temptation will form the crisis of your disease. If your spiritual constitution can sustain it, you recover; if not, you die.[5]

God knows there are times to flee and times to stand. As John Bunyan said, "There are few rules in this case. The man himself is best able to judge concerning his present strength, and what weight this or that argument has upon his heart to stand or fly."[6] Bunyan, who spent twelve years in prison, when a simple pledge not to preach would have provided his freedom, has written compassionately and biblically about the tension between flying for safety and standing to suffer. To the question *May we try to escape?* Bunyan answers,

> Thou mayest do in this as it is in thy heart. If it is in thy heart to fly, fly: if it be in thy heart to stand, stand. Any thing but a denial of the truth. He that flies, has warrant to do so; he that stands, has warrant to do so. Yea, the same man may both fly and stand, as the call and working of God with his heart may be. Moses fled, Ex. 2:15; Moses stood. Heb. 11:27. David fled, 1 Sam. 19:12; David stood. 24:8. Jeremiah fled, Je. 37:11–12; Jeremiah stood. 38:17. Christ withdrew himself, Luke 9:10; Christ stood. John 18:1–8. Paul fled, 2 Cor. 11:33; Paul stood. Acts 20:22–23. . . .
>
> There are few rules in this case. The man himself is best able to judge concerning his present strength, and what weight this or that argument has upon his heart to stand or

---

[5]"Advice to Missionary Candidates by Adoniram Judson," http://www.wholesomewords.org/missions/bjudson4.html; accessed 05-17-08.

[6]John Bunyan, *Seasonable Counsels, or Advice to Sufferers,* in *Works,* Vol. 2, ed. George Offor (Edinburgh: The Banner of Truth Trust, 1991, reprinted from the 1854 edition published by W. G. Blackie and Son, Glasgow), p. 726.

fly. . . . Do not fly out of a slavish fear, but rather because flying is an ordinance of God, opening a door for the escape of some, which door is opened by God's providence, and the escape countenanced by God's Word. Matt. 10:23.

If, therefore, when thou hast fled, thou art taken, be not offended at God or man: not at God, for thou art his servant, thy life and thy all are his; not at man, for he is but God's rod, and is ordained, in this, to do thee good. Hast thou escaped? Laugh. Art thou taken? Laugh. I mean, be pleased which way soever things shall go, for that the scales are still in God's hand. [7]

My hope for this book is that our hearts and minds have been shaped more deeply by the work of the Spirit so that when the crisis comes, we will be guided more by the ways of God and less by the worldly assumptions of security and comfort.

How Likely the Crisis of Martyrdom?

Indeed, I pray that the backbone of our courage would be steeled by these stories of faithfulness so that when the necessity of martyrdom comes, we would be ready. How likely is that crisis? It depends on where you live and where you are willing to go.

Each year David Barrett, Todd Johnson, and Peter Crossing publish their annual "Status of Global Mission, Presence, and Activities, AD 1800-2025." One of the most sobering items in this seventy-nine-item report is called "Average Christian Martyrs per Year." The global number for 2008 was 175,000. That's 479 Christians every day who lost their lives as a result of being a Christian.

These are not martyrs who die at their own hands like so

---

[7]Ibid.

many jihadists who kill others as they kill themselves. That is not the way of Jesus. Followers of Christ do not kill in order to spread the gospel about Christ who died so that his enemies could live. Christian martyrdom is not suicide. But it is willingly accepted if necessary.

Judson loved life and cherished three wives and all his children. He exercised faithfully to preserve health and life. He told missionary candidates, "Beware of that indolence which leads to a neglect of bodily exercise. The poor health and premature death of most Europeans in the East must be eminently ascribed to the most wanton neglect of bodily exercise."[8]

Paton faced down fierce opposition at the risk of his life again and again, but also chose to flee from hundreds of crazed enemies by hiding in a tree and finding a boat to get off the island of Tanna. He was not eager to die. He wanted to spend his long life evangelizing the New Hebrides. And he was granted his heart's desire. He was eighty-two when he died.

Tyndale did not want to die. He was only forty-two. He had not yet married. He was in a foreign land. His cause was just. He was a promising scholar and preacher. But when the decision was rendered that he would be burned, he accepted it as the will of God. He was imbued with the spirit of 1 Peter 4:19: "Let those who suffer according to God's will entrust their souls to a faithful Creator while doing good."

This was the pattern for thousands of frontline peacemakers from the earliest times to this very day. For example, on July 17, 180, in one of the Roman provinces of Africa, six Christians were put on trial for refusing to render full homage to the Emperor,

---

[8]"Advice to Missionary Candidates by Adoniram Judson," http://www.wholesomewords.org/missions/bjudson4.html; accessed 05-17-08.

even though they kept the laws and paid their taxes. Their names were Speratus, Nartzalus, Cittinus, Donata, Secunda, and Vestia. They were being tried by proconsul Saturninus along with others. The dialogue of their last hours was recorded:

> The proconsul Saturninus said: "Have no part in this madness."
>
> Cittinus said: "We have none other to fear save the Lord our God who is in heaven."
>
> Donata said: "Give honor to Caesar as unto Caesar, but fear to God."
>
> Vestia said: "I am a Christian."
>
> Secunda said: "I wish to be none other than what I am."
>
> The proconsul Saturninus said to Speratus: "Do you persist in remaining a Christian?"
>
> Speratus said: "I am a Christian." And all were of one mind with him.
>
> The proconsul Saturninus said: "Do you desire any space for consideration?"
>
> Speratus said: "When the right is so clear there is nothing to consider."
>
> The proconsul Saturninus said: "What have you in your case?"
>
> Speratus said: "The Books, and the letters of a just man, one Paul."
>
> The proconsul Saturninus said: " Take a reprieve of thirty days and think it over."
>
> Speratus again said: "I am a Christian." And all were of one mind with him.
>
> The proconsul Saturninus read out the sentence from his notebook: "Whereas Speratus, Nartzalus, Cittinus, Donata, Vestia, Secunda, and the rest have confessed that they live in accordance with the religious rites of the Christians, and,

when an opportunity was given them of returning to the usage of the Romans, persevered in their obstinacy, it is our pleasure that they should suffer by the sword."

Speratus said: "Thanks be to God."

Nartzalus said: "Today we are martyrs in heaven: thanks be to God!"

The proconsul Saturninus commanded that proclamation be made by the herald: "I have commanded that Speratus, Nartzalus, Cittinus, Veturius, Felix, Aquilinus, Laetantius, Januaria, Generosa, Vestia, Donata, Secunda be led forth to execution."

They all said: "Thanks be to God!"

And so all were crowned with martyrdom together, and reign with the Father and the Son and the Holy Spirit for ever and ever. Amen.[9]

How the Death of Martyrs Blossoms

How likely is the crisis of martyrdom today? Perhaps a better question is: How important is martyrdom today? How important is suffering for the sake of taking the gospel to the nations? George Otis Jr. shocked many at the Second Lausanne Congress on World Evangelization in Manila in 1989 when he asked, "Is our failure to thrive in Muslim countries owing to the absence of martyrs? Can a covert church grow in strength? Does a young church need martyr models?"

Fittingly he concludes his book *The Last of the Giants* with a chapter entitled "Risk Safety."

Should the Church in politically or socially trying circumstances remain covert to avoid potential eradication

---

[9]"The Martyrs of Scilli in Africa Proconsularis, 17 July 180," in J. Stevenson, ed., *A New Eusebius: Documents Illustrative of the History of the Church to A. D. 337* (London: SPCK, 1968), pp. 41–42.

by forces hostile to Christianity? Or would more open confrontation with prevailing spiritual ignorance and deprivation—even if it produced Christian martyrs— be more likely to lead to evangelistic breakthroughs? Islamic fundamentalists claim that their spiritual revolution is fueled by the blood of martyrs. Is it conceivable that Christianity's failure to thrive in the Muslim world is due to the notable absence of Christian martyrs? And can the Muslim community take seriously the claims of a Church in hiding? . . . The question is not whether it is wise at times to keep worship and witness discreet, but rather how long this may continue before we are guilty of "hiding our light under a bushel." . . . The record shows that from Jerusalem and Damascus to Ephesus and Rome, the apostles were beaten, stoned, conspired against and imprisoned for their witness. Invitations were rare, and never the basis for their missions.[10]

Otis would have agreed with Gregory the Great (pope from 590 to 604) when he said, "The death of the martyrs blossoms in the lives of the faithful."[11]

None of this is without divine meaning and design. God saved us by the suffering and death of his Son. It is his pattern to send this message of salvation to the world by displaying a realistic picture of those sufferings in the suffering of his servants. The reason for this pattern is to make clear to us and to the world that the surpassing and successful effect of this mission belongs to God and not to us. Paul shows us this divine purpose through his own life:

---

[10]George Otis Jr., *The Last of the Giants: Lifting the Veil on Islam and the End Times* (Grand Rapids, MI: Chosen Books, 1991), pp. 261, 263. This account of George Otis at Lausanne is based on my own notes from being there and hearing him. I recorded this also in *Desiring God: Meditations of a Christian Hedonist* (Sisters, OR: Multnomah, 2003), p. 273.
[11]Quoted in Joseph Tson, "A Theology of Martyrdom" (an undated booklet of The Romanian Missionary Society, Wheaton, IL), p. 1.

> We were so utterly burdened beyond our strength that
> we despaired of life itself. Indeed, we felt that we had
> received the sentence of death. But *that was to make us
> rely not on ourselves but on God* who raises the dead. . . .
> But we have this treasure in jars of clay, to show that
> *the surpassing power belongs to God* and not to us. . . .
> "*My power* is made perfect in weakness." (2 Corinthians
> 1:8–9; 4:7; 12:9).

In the end, the message, the method, and the final outcome of missions will all work together to make us humbly dependent on God, and to show God graciously powerful to save. If we must suffer along the way to put Christ's sacrificial love on display, it will be a small price for the inheritance to come. "I consider that the sufferings of this present time are not worth comparing with the glory that is to be revealed to us" (Romans 8:18). "This light momentary affliction is preparing for us an eternal weight of glory beyond all comparison" (2 Corinthians 4:17).

Walk Softly to the Nations

Therefore, we may receive Adoniram Judson's final counsel with peace. After observing that "a large proportion of those who come out on a mission to the East die within five years," he says, "Walk softly, therefore; death is narrowly watching your steps."[12]

Indeed, death is watching our steps. We are as fragile as a flower that fades. Let there be no triumphalistic swagger. No cocky self-assurance. Let us accept humbly that we are "a mist

---

[12] "Advice to Missionary Candidates by Adoniram Judson," http://www.wholesomewords.org/missions/bjudson4.html; accessed 5-17-08.

that appears for a little time and then vanishes" (James 4:14). And let us resolve to set our faces like flint on the path of obedience and never turn back. And with a full grasp of the possible cost before us, and with full courage because of Christ, let us walk softly to every unreached people that remains.

SCRIPTURE INDEX

PERSON INDEX

à Kempis, Thomas, 100
Abraham (Aneityumese servant), 61-
  62, 68, 69, 74, 78-79
Anderson, Courtney, 85, 88-95, 97-
  100, 102-106
Arundell, Thomas, 44
Athanasius, Bishop, 41
Augustine, Aurelius, 9

Bainham, James, 45
Bale, John, 44
Barrett, David, 86, 112
Barth, Karl, 42
Barton, Elizabeth, 46
Bayfield, Richard, 45
Bell, Ralph, 57
Bellamy, Joseph, 87
Bent, John, 45
Bilney, Thomas, 45
Boardman, George, 102
Bunyan, John, 111

Calvin, John, 8, 42
Carey, William, 85, 93
Chubbuck, Emily, 105-106
Cittinus, 113-115
Cook, James, 53
Coverdale, Miles, 32
Cowper, William, 98
Cromwell, Thomas, 27
Crossing, Peter, 112

Daniell, David, 27-35, 37-44, 46-48,
  50-52
de Quiros, Fernandez, 53

Dennis, Lane, 11
Dickson, Mr., 58

Donaldson, James, 25
Donata, 113-115
Dusgate, Thomas, 45

Eames, Jacob, 90, 91
Edwards, Jonathan, 87
Eraclius, 9
Erasmus, 29, 36-42

Fenelon, François de Salignac de la
  Mothe, 100
Forester, Fanny, 105
Foxe, John, 30, 44, 48-49, 52
Frith, John, 45, 52

Geddie, John, 54
Gordon, Mr. and Mrs. G. N., 65,
  77, 79
Guyon, Madame, 100

Hall, Gordon, 93
Harding, Thomas, 45-46
Harris, James, 53, 58, 77
Harrison, Eugene Myers, 87
Henry VIII, King, 27-29
Hewet, Andrew, 46
Hulse, Erroll, 87

Inglis, John, 54

James, King, 32
Jerome, St., 44
Johnson, Todd, 112
Johnstone, Patrick, 86, 109
Jones, Emrys, 37
Judson, Abigail Brown (mother),
  89, 96

SUBJECT INDEX

✳ desiringGod

If you would like to further explore the vision of God and life presented in this book, we at Desiring God would love to serve you. We have hundreds of resources to help you grow in your passion for Jesus Christ and help you spread that passion to others. At our website, desiringGod.org, you'll find almost everything John Piper has written and preached, including more than thirty books. We've made over twenty-five years of his sermons available free online for you to read, listen to, download, and in some cases watch.

In addition, you can access hundreds of articles, listen to our daily internet radio program, find out where John Piper is speaking, learn about our conferences, discover our God-centered children's curricula, and browse our online store. John Piper receives no royalties from the books he writes and no compensation from Desiring God. The funds are all reinvested into our gospel-spreading efforts. DG also has a whatever-you-can-afford policy, designed for individuals with limited discretionary funds. If you'd like more information about this policy, please contact us at the address or phone number below. We exist to help you treasure Jesus Christ and his gospel above all things because he is most glorified in you when you are most satisfied in him. Let us know how we can serve you!

Desiring God
Post Office Box 2901
Minneapolis, Minnesota 55402

888.346.4700
mail@desiringGod.org
www.desiringGod.org